Printed in China

Morality

道德篇

李小艳　陈爱明　编译

林　立　　　审校

外文出版社

卷首语

总有一种感动无处不在。

总有一种情怀轻舞飞扬。

总有一种生活，在别处，闪动异样的光芒。

阅读，让我们的生活在情调与知性中享受更多……

故事与见闻，犹处生活的魅力与智慧，合着我们自身生命的光与影，陪伴我们一路前行。

快乐和圆满，幻想与失落，飞扬的眼泪，

行走江湖的落拓，不与人说的痛苦，渐行渐远的繁华，坚持的勇气，点点滴滴的小意思……

人生让我们感受到的，也许远远不只是这些；更多的是挫折后生长的力量，沉闷时的豁然开朗，是屋前那静静的南山上盛开的人淡如菊的境界，是闹市中跋涉红尘、豪情万丈的冲动，是很纯粹的一杯午后的香醇的咖啡……

漫步红尘，有彻悟来自他人的故事，有灵犀来自偶然的相遇，在这里，一种从未见过的却可能早就在我们心底的生活方式有可能与我们邂逅。

让我们一起阅读吧，感受生长的智慧、风雅与力量。

Contents
目　　录

The beggar's wish

乞丐的愿望

He felt he should ask for all the things he missed in life.

他觉得自己应该要生命中该有而没有的一切东西。

A beggar who had been blind was very devoted[1] and used to worship regularly at a certain shrine[2]. At the same time, he would empty his bowl of whatever amount of coins he received through begging and offered them to the shrine. The priest in charge of the shrine noticed the beggar's devotion, and, wishing to encourage him, said one day.

"Oh, beggar, the gods are pleased with your devotion and gifts. They say that they will bestow[3] upon you whatever single gift you may ask for. But remember you may ask for one thing only."

The beggar was delighted to hear such a wonderful message. He immediately thought what particular gift he should ask for. But the more he thought the more confused he became for there were so many things he felt he needed — sight, wealth, long life, a wife, children, and so on.

But he was a clever man and after much serious meditation[4], he felt he should ask for all the things he missed in life. He then went to the shrine and said to the priest:

"Oh, holy one, I thank you for intervening with the gods to bestow upon me one gift. I am now about to ask for one thing and one thing only."

"Say it out loud, and your wish will be granted," cried the holy man to the beggar.

一个双目失明的乞丐很虔诚，过去经常定期地去某个圣祠朝拜。同时，他总是把他乞讨到的所有的钱都投进木箱。管理圣祠的神父看到乞丐的捐赠，于是有一天以鼓励的口吻对他说道：

"喂，乞丐。诸神看到你的虔诚和礼物很高兴，他们说无论你要求什么，他们都会赐给你的。但是切记你只能要一件东西。"

乞丐听到这话很高兴。他马上开始考虑应该要什么礼物。可是他越想越不知道要什么好，因为他需要的东西太多了——恢复视力、财富、长寿、妻子、孩子等等。

然而，乞丐很聪明，经过一番仔细考虑之后，他觉得自己应该要生命中该有而没有的一切东西。于是就到圣祠对神父说：

"尊敬的神父，我很感谢您向诸神要求赐予我一件礼物。现在我想要一件东西，就一件。"

"说出来吧，你的愿望会实现的。"神父对乞丐说。

❶ devoted
/dɪˈvəʊtɪd/
adj. 虔诚

❷ shrine
/ʃraɪn/
n. 圣祠

❸ bestow
/bɪˈstəʊ/
v. 赐予

❹ meditation
/medɪˈteɪʃən/
n. 考虑

"Well, my petition[5] is simple. Before I die that I may see my son's grandson living in a six-storied house, drinking milk and honey and eating fragrant rice out of a golden bowl."

In this way the clever beggar had really asked for sight, family, wealth, a palace, longevity and happiness and his wish was granted.

"好吧，我的愿望很简单。在我死之前，我想看到我的曾孙住在六层高的大房子里，喝着牛奶和蜂蜜，用金碗吃着香喷喷的饭菜。"

就这样，这个聪明的乞丐实际上要的是视力、家庭、财富、豪宅、长寿和幸福，他的愿望实现了。

❺ petition

/pɪˈtɪʃən/

n. 请求

Everyone agrees to peace

人人都赞同和平

Haven't you heard?   Everyone has agreed to live in peace.

你没有听人说过吗？每个人都愿意和平地生活。

A sly fox tried to trick[1] a rooster into coming down from his perch[2].

"Brother Bird," the fox said, "come down and have a friendly chat!"

"No," said the rooster, "I'm sure you'd eat me."

"Oh, I wouldn't," said the crafty fox, "Haven't you heard? Everyone has agreed to live in peace."

"Is that so?" said rooster, who was just as crafty.

Stretching his neck, the rooster pretended to look at something far off in the distance.

"What are you looking at?" asked the fox curiously.

"Oh...Just a pack of hungry fox hounds headed right this way."

Upon hearing this, the fox trembled in his tracks and ran off.

"Come back!" crowed the rooster, "Why are you running away? I thought you said that everyone has agreed to live in peace."

"Well, perhaps those hungry hounds haven't heard about it yet," said the fox, and he bounded[3] away.

一只狡猾的狐狸想把一只公鸡从栖息的树枝上骗下来。

"公鸡兄弟"，狐狸说，"下来我们好好地聊一聊吧。"

"不！"公鸡说，"你肯定要吃了我。"

"哦，不会的。"狡猾的狐狸说。"你没有听人说过吗？每个人都愿意和平地生活。"

"真的吗？"公鸡说。它和狐狸一样精明。

公鸡伸长脖子，假装看了看远处的东西。

"你在看什么？"狐狸好奇地问。

"哦，有一群饥饿的猎狗正朝这边跑过来了。"

一听到这话，狐狸就吓得直哆嗦，赶快跑开了。

"回来！"公鸡叫道，"你为什么跑啊？你不是说每个人都愿意和平地生活啊。"

"可能那些饥饿的猎狗还没听过这句话吧！"狐狸说着就拼命地跑开了。

❶ trick
/trɪk/
v. 骗

❷ perch
/pɜːtʃ/
n. 栖木

❸ bound
/baʊnd/
v. 惊慌失措地跑

The banquet

宴 会

But it was these clothes that brought me all this food.

但是正是这些衣服给我带来所有这些食物。

A poor man dressed in rags came to the palace to attend the banquet. Out of courtesy he was admitted but, because of his tattered[1] clothing, he was seated at the very end of the banquet table. By the time the platters arrived at his seat, there was no food left on them.

So he left the banquet, returning several hours later dressed in robes and jewels he had borrowed from a wealthy friend. This time he was brought immediately to the head of the table and, with great ceremony, food was brought to his seat first.

"Oh, what delicious food I see being served upon my plate." He rubbed one spoonful into his clothes for every one he ate.

A nobleman beside him, grimacing[2] at the mess, inquired, "Sir, why are you rubbing food into your fine clothes?"

"Oh," he replied with a chuckle[3], "Pardon me if my robes now look the worst. But it was these clothes that brought me all this food. It's only fair that they be fed first!"

一个衣衫褴褛的穷人去宫殿参加宴会，门卫出于礼貌让他进去了。但是因为他破旧的衣服，他被安排坐在宴会桌的最尽头，等到盛食物的盘子传到他时，已经没剩下什么了。

于是他离开宫殿，几个小时后又回来了，穿着礼袍、戴着宝石，这些东西都是他从一个富有的朋友那儿借来的。这次他立刻被带到贵宾席，食物以隆重的仪式最先端到他的面前。

"哦，这些菜真是美味佳肴啊。"他每吃一口就往他精美的衣服上抹一勺。

他旁边坐着一个高贵的人，看到这么恶心的举动露出痛苦的表情，问道："先生，为什么往你精美的衣服上抹食物呢？"

"哦"，他笑着回答，"如果礼袍看起来太脏了，请原谅我，但是正是这些衣服给我带来所有这些食物，所以先给它们吃才公平啊。"

❶ tattered
/'tæted/
adj. 破旧的
❷ grimace
/grɪ'meɪs/
v. 露出痛苦的表情
❸ chuckle
/'tʃʌkəl/
v. 轻声地说笑

The warrior and his sons

勇士和他的儿子们

A man is never truly dead until he is forgotten!

一个人只有被遗忘时才真正地死亡了。

A great warrior[1] did not return from the hunt. His family gave him up for dead, all except his youngest child who each day would ask, "Where is my father? Where is my father?"

The child's older brothers, who were magicians[2], finally went forth to find him. They came upon his broken spear[3] and a pile of bones. The first son assembled the bones into a skeleton; the second son put flesh upon the bones; the third son breathed life into the flesh.

The warrior arose and walked into the village where there was great celebration. He said, "I will give a fine gift to the one who has brought me back to life."

Each one of his sons cried out, "Give it to me, for I have done the most."

"I will give the gift to my youngest child," said the warrior. "For it is this child who saved my life. A man is never truly dead until he is forgotten!"

一位勇士出征未归，他的家人都以为他死了，只有他最小的儿子每天都问："爸爸哪去了？爸爸在哪儿？"

小孩的几个哥哥都是魔法师，最后他们决定去找爸爸。他们找到了他的断矛，还有一堆骨头。第一个儿子把骨头组装成骨架，第二个儿子把肉附在骨头上，第三个儿子吹了口气让肌肉恢复了生命。

勇士站起身，走进村子，加入到欢庆会中。他说："我要给帮我恢复生命的人一件精美的礼物。"

他的儿子们都喊道："给我吧，我出的力最大！"

"我将把这个礼物给小儿子，"勇士说，"因为他救了我的命。一个人只有被遗忘时才真正地死亡了。"

❶ warrior
/ˈwɒrɪə/
n. 武士，勇士
❷ magician
/məˈdʒɪʃən/
n. 魔法师
❸ spear
/spɪə/
n. 矛

The girl and her bucket

女孩和桶

My dreams are splattered in puddles of milk on the road ...

我的梦想就这样随着牛奶洒落一地而破灭了……

A young girl was going to market with a bucket of milk on her head.

"With the gold that I get from the sale of this milk, I'll buy a red hen," she said. "The hen will lay eggs, they'll hatch and then I'll have many chicks to raise. I'll feed them well and when they are grown, they will each lay eggs. and those eggs will hatch and I will have more hens, who'll lay more eggs that will hatch into chicks...

Before long I'll be rich and I'll wear fine clothes with emeralds[1] and rubies[2] from my collar to my toes and one day perhaps I shall visit the Queen. I shall bring her rare gifts from China. I'll enter the court with my arms full of treasure. Bowing low I shall say, 'FOR YOUR MAJESTY'S PLEASURE!'"

And she bowed low...

With that sweep of her arm, she knocked off the bucket and spilled her fantasy load.

"Oh dear," she cried, "my dreams are splattered[3] in puddles[4] of milk on the road..."

一个小女孩顶着一桶牛奶到集市上去卖。

"卖了这桶牛奶后，我要买一只红母鸡。"她想。"母鸡会下蛋，也可以孵蛋，那样我就可以养很多小鸡。我把它们好好地喂养大，到时候它们就会下蛋，那些蛋又孵化成小鸡，然后我就有更多的母鸡下蛋，再孵小鸡……"

"不久我就会很富有，我要穿上精美的衣服，从脖子到脚都镶着祖母绿宝石和红宝石，可能有一天我会去拜访王后，从中国给她带去珍贵的礼物。我要走进宫廷，手捧着金银珠宝，向她鞠躬问好：'女王陛下！'"

她还真深深地鞠躬了。

她举手行礼时，把寄予无限幻想的牛奶打翻了。

"哦，天哪！"她叫道，"我的梦想就这样随着牛奶洒落一地而破灭了……"

❶ emerald
/ˈemərəld/
n. 祖母绿
❷ ruby
/ˈruːbɪ/
n. 红宝石
❸ splatter
/ˈsplætə/
v. 溅泼
❹ puddle
/ˈpʌdl/
n. 坑洼

The lion and the rabbit

狮子和兔子

The first to go to the lion's den was a timid rabbit, who went slowly.

第一个到狮子洞穴的是一只胆小的兔子。

The animals of the forest made a bargain with a ferocious[1] lion who killed for pleasure. It was agreed that one animal each day would willingly come to the ferocious lion's den to be his supper and, in turn, the lion would never hunt again. The first to go to the lion's den was a timid rabbit, who went slowly.

"Why are you late?" the lion roared when the rabbit arrived.

"I'm late because of the other lion," said the rabbit.

"In my jungle? Take me to this other lion."

The rabbit led the lion to a deep well and told him to look in. The lion saw his own reflection[2] in the water and roared! The sound of his roar bounced right back at him as an echo.

"I alone am king of this jungle," he roared again.

His echo answered him, "I alone am king of this jungle."

With that, the lion became so enraged[3], he charged into the deep well with a great splash! The lion attacked his own reflection and was never heard from again.

森里里的动物和以追杀为乐的狮子进行谈判，最后达成了协议：每天依次有一个动物自愿到凶猛的狮子那里去作他的晚餐，这样狮子就再也不准追杀其他动物。第一个去狮子洞穴的是一只胆小的兔子。

"你为什么迟到了？"兔子到达时，狮子吼道。

"我迟到是因为遇到其他的狮子了。"兔子说。

"在我的森里里？带我去看看那只狮子。"

兔子把狮子带到一个深井旁叫他往里面看，狮子看见水里的倒影，咆哮起来。咆哮之后有回声传回来。

"我是这片森林惟一的国王。"他又怒吼道。

回声回答说："我是这片森林惟一的国王。"

听到这话，狮子变得非常恼怒，他扑向深井，井里溅起很大的水花，狮子跳下去袭击他自己的倒影了。从此之后再也没有听到狮子的消息。

❶ ferocious
/fəˈrəʊʃəs/
adj. 凶猛的
❷ reflection
/rɪˈflekʃən/
n. 倒影
❸ enrage
/ɪnˈreɪdʒ/
v. 激怒

Lady Godiva

戈蒂维夫人

He thought the Lady would be ashamed to expose her naked body and that she would not take up the challenge.

他以为夫人会太羞于显露自己的裸体而不接受挑战。

A long time ago, there was a rich man called Lord of Coventry. He had a beautiful wife called Lady Godiva. She was greatly beloved by the people for her many gracious services to the sick and the poor.

When the Lord wanted to increase taxes on the townsfolk, they sought the help of Lady Godiva. They implored[1] her to intercede[2] on their behalf to her husband to reduce the taxes.

Accordingly, Lady Godiva pleaded with the Lord but he roughly refused except on one condition. "Alright my Lady," he said smiling cynically[3], "if you consent to ride through the town clothed in naught but your loosened hair you shall have your way, but not otherwise."

It was a hard condition which only a bully of a husband could impose. He thought the Lady would be ashamed to expose her naked body and that she would not take up the challenge.

But Lady Godiva was determined to trust and help her loving people even at such a cost to her pride and modesty. The Lady sent word to the townsfolk of her bargain with the Lord.

On the following morning, as Lady Godiva rode from end to end of the town of Coventry, all the townsfolk remained indoors with their doors tightly shut, so as not to cause their benefactor[4] any shame or embarrassment.

很久以前，有一位富有的考文垂伯爵，他美丽的妻子戈蒂维夫人深受人民爱戴，因为她对患病或贫穷的人们总是慷慨解囊。

伯爵想向镇民多征税，镇民们无奈，只好去求助于戈蒂维夫人，求她代他们向她的伯爵丈夫求情减少税收。

于是，戈蒂维夫人向伯爵求情，却遭到了粗暴的拒绝，除非答应他一个条件。"好吧，我的夫人，"他笑了笑，带着嘲讽的口气说："如果你同意不穿衣服、披着头发，骑着马在镇上走一趟，我就答应你，但是，其他方式都不行。"

只有虐待狂丈夫才会提出这样苛刻的条件。他以为夫人会太羞于显露自己的裸体而不接受挑战。

但是，戈蒂维夫人决定信任并帮助爱戴她的人民，即使以她的尊严和庄重为代价也在所不惜。夫人派人把她与伯爵的谈判告诉了镇民们。

第二天早上，戈蒂维夫人骑马从考文垂镇的一头走到另一头时，所有镇民都待在家里，紧闭门窗，以免让他们的恩人蒙羞或感到尴尬。

伯爵信守了诺言，镇民的税收负担免除了。直到今天，考文垂的市民们都发自内心

❶ implore
/ɪmˈplɔː/
v. 恳求

❷ intercede
/ˌɪntəˈsiːd/
v. 调解

❸ cynically
/ˈsɪnɪkəlɪ/
adv. 嘲讽地

❹ benefactor
/ˈbenɪfæktə/
n. 恩人

The Lord kept his word to his wife. The tax burden of the people was removed and to this day, the citizens of Coventry delight to do honor to the memory of this great Lady Godiva. This incident took place in 1040. Lady Godiva with her long hair flowing loosely while riding naked on a horse was also known as The Lady in White.

Moral: All ladies should be proud to remember the courage and sacrifice of Lady Godiva. She did this not for fame or money but for the love of her people.

地尊敬这位伟大的戈蒂维夫人。这是发生在1040 年的真实的故事，长发飘飘、裸体骑在马背上的戈蒂维夫人也被称作是"白衣女子"。

寓意：所有女士都应为戈蒂维夫人表现上的勇气和牺牲精神而骄傲。她这样做不是为了名誉或金钱，而是为了她对人民的爱。

Home

家

An artist who had painted many pictures of great beauty found that he had not yet painted the one "real" picture.

一位画家画了许多精美的画之后，发现自己并没有画出一幅"真实"的画。

An artist who had painted many pictures of great beauty found that he had not yet painted the one "real" picture.

In his search along a dusty road, he met an aged priest who asked him where he was going. "I do not know," said the artist, "I want to paint the most beautiful thing in the world. Perhaps you can direct me to it."

"How simple," replied the priest, "in any church or creed, you will find it — 'Faith' is the most beautiful thing in the world."

The artist traveled on. Later, he met a young bride who told him that the most beautiful thing in the world is "Love." "Love" makes the world go round. It builds poverty into riches, sweetens tears and makes much of little. Without love there is no beauty.

Still the artist continued his search and met a weary[1] soldier. The artist asked him the same question and the soldier answered, "Peace" is the most beautiful thing in the world. War is ugly and wherever you find peace you'll find beauty, faith and love.

"How can I paint them — Faith, Love and Peace?" thought the artist. As he resumed[2] his walk, his mind wondered on the "real" picture he hoped to paint. He was surprised that without thinking where he was going, he had reached his familiar surrounding. As he entered the doorway, light glistened[3] in his eyes and he realized that his search was over.

一位画家画了许多精美的画之后，发现自己并没有画出一幅"真实"的画。

他沿着一条尘土飞扬的路寻找着，遇到一位年老的牧师问他要去哪里。"我不知道，"画家说，"我想画出世界上最美的东西。说不定你能够指点我。"

"多简单啊，"牧师说，"在任何一座教堂里或任何一条教义中都能找到——'信仰'就是世界上最美的东西。"

画家继续前行。后来，他碰见一个年轻的新郎，新郎告诉他说世界上最美的东西是"爱"。"爱"使世界运转起来。它使贫穷变得富有，使泪水变得甜蜜，使点滴变得巨大。没有爱，就没有美。

画家仍然继续寻找，遇到了一名疲乏的士兵，画家问了他同样的问题，士兵回答："'和平'是世界上最美的东西。战争是丑恶的，找到了和平即找到了美、信仰和爱。"

"我怎样才能把它们——信仰、爱和和平画出来呢？"画家想。他又上路了，脑子里思忖着他希望画出来的"真实的"画。根本没有想自己在往哪里走，他惊奇地发现自己竟来到了熟悉的地方。进门时，闪烁的灯光映入眼帘，他意识到自己的寻找结束了。

❶ weary
/ˈwɪərɪ/
adj. 疲劳的
❷ resume
/rɪˈzjuːm/
v. 再继续
❸ glisten
/glzsn/
v. 发光

In the faces of his wife and children, he saw Love and Faith. "Not a minute passed by that our children and I had not thought of you. We prayed that you would return to us safely," his wife said as they embraced[4] him. He sat on his favorite old chair and his heart was at peace.

The artist painted the most beautiful thing in the world and called it "HOME".

Moral: No matter where we may roam[5], there's no place like home.

在妻子和孩子们的脸上，他看见了爱和信仰。"在这段时间里，我和孩子们无时无刻不在想着你。我们祈祷你安然无恙地回到我们身边。"说着，他们拥抱在一起。他坐在最喜欢的古椅上，心情无比平静。

画家画出了最美的东西，把它叫做《家》。

寓意：东好西好，不如自己的家好。

❹ embrace
/ɪmˈbreɪs/
v. 拥抱

❺ roam
/rəʊm/
v. 漫游；闲逛

Two mothers and a baby
两位母亲和一个孩子

No real mother could bear to see her child cut into half.

没有哪个真正的母亲会忍心看着自己的孩子被劈成两半的。

It happened a long time ago in a small native village in China. There were two brothers living in the same house. Both sisters-in-law were expecting[1]. The elder woman who had a miscarriage[2] did not let anyone know about it. When both women were in confinement[3] and the younger sister-in-law delivered a baby boy, the elder one stole her child at night.

For three years the two mothers were fighting over the baby. Each claimed that the little baby was hers. The matter was brought before a chief minister of the county. As he listened to their story, he said: "Since there's only one baby, I don't see how I can give him to either one of you. The best thing I can do is to cut the baby into half. Each can take one-half of the baby."

The elder lady smiled and quickly replied, "Sir, I accept your decision." But the younger sister-in-law lady cried and begged the chief minister saying, "Please sir, don't cut the baby into half. Let her have the baby! "

When the verdict[4] a was made, the chief minister gave the baby to the mother who was willing to "sacrifice" her baby and give her up to the older lady. "No real mother could bear to see her child cut into half." he pronounced.

Moral: Sacrifice is real love.

很久以前，在中国的一个小村子里，有兄弟两家人住在同一所房子里，妯娌两个都有了身孕。嫂子小产，却没有让任何人知道。两个女人分娩之后，弟妹生了一个男孩，嫂子在夜里把孩子偷走了。

三年来，两位母亲一直在为孩子是谁的而争吵，她们都说小孩是自己的。事情闹到了县衙门。县令听完故事说："既然只有一个孩子，我不知道到底该把他给你们哪一个。我能做的最好的事就是把孩子劈成两半，每人得一半。"

嫂子笑了笑，立即回答说："大人，我同意您的决定。"但是，弟妹却哭着求县令说："大人，请不要把孩子劈成两半，把孩子给她吧！"

县令做出裁决，孩子属于宁愿放弃孩子、把他让给嫂子的那位母亲。"没有哪个真正的母亲会忍心看着自己的孩子被劈成两半的。"他说。

寓意：牺牲即真爱。

❶ **expect**
/ɪkˈspekt/
adj. 怀孕

❷ **miscarriage**
/mɪsˈkærɪdʒ/
n. 小产

❸ **confinement**
/kənˈfaɪnmənt/
n. 分娩

❹ **verdict**
/ˈvɜːdɪkt/
n. 裁决

The boatman

船　夫

In that case, you've wasted all your life.

那样的话，你浪费了整个生命。

A scholar asked a boatman to row him across the river. The journey was long and slow. The scholar was bored. "Boatman," he called out, "Let's have a conversation." Suggesting a topic of special interest to himself, he asked, "Have you ever studied phonetics or grammar? "

"No," said the boatman, "I've no use for those tools."

"Too bad," said the scholar, "You've wasted half your life. It's useful to know the rules."

Later, as the rickety[1] boat crashed into a rock in the middle of the river, the boatman turned to the scholar and said, "Pardon my humble mind that to you must seem dim[2], but, wise man, tell me, have you ever learned to swim? "

"No," said the scholar, "I've never learned. I've immersed[3] myself in thinking."

"In that case, " said the boatman, "you've wasted all your life. Alas, the boat is sinking!"

一个学者让一个船夫渡他过河，这次行程既长又慢，学者无聊了。"船夫，"他叫道，"我们聊聊天吧。"他提出一个他自己非常感兴趣的话题问道："你研究过语音学或者语法吗？"

"没有，"船夫说，"我研究那玩意没用。"

"太遗憾了，"学者说道，"你浪费了你一半的生命。知道那些规则是很有用的。"

过了一会，摇摇晃晃的船撞到河中间的一块石头上，船夫转向学者对他说："请原谅，在你看来我的脑袋是多么的愚笨，但是，聪明人，告诉我，你学过游泳吗？"

"没有，"学者答道，"我从来没学过，我一直都专心于思考。"

"那样的话，"船夫说，"你浪费了整个生命。瞧，船正在下沉呢！"

❶ rickety
/ˈrɪkɪtɪ/
adj. 摇摆的
❷ dim
/dɪm/
adj. 愚笨的
❸ immerse
/ɪˈmɜːs/
v. 专心于

Why was the green caterpillar so happy?

绿毛虫为何如此快乐？

But whatever you think, the ugly Green Caterpillar had to sleep and wait its turn before it became a butterfly.

但是，不管你怎样想，丑陋的绿毛虫都要等待时机才能变成蝴蝶。

There once lived a little Green Caterpillar[1] who was very happy. And why should he not be happy? The great golden sun shone down brightly upon him. The flowers nodded gracefully[2] as the mild wind blew pleasantly. The birds sang "twit twit twit" sweetly. Best of all, the waving grasses tasted, oh, so good, for little Green Caterpillar was always hungry.

"You are very ugly, Little Green Caterpillar and very lazy too," said the ants as they passed by. "All day long you lie in the sunshine and do nothing!" Little Green Caterpillar looked up and smiled but went on eating.

Mr Bumble Bee stopped with a message from the Spider, the spinner. Mr Bumble Bee could not help but told Little Green Caterpillar how ugly he was. But Little Green Caterpillar did not take any notice of his comment and went on eating.

A group of butterflies passed by on their way to the Butterfly Ball. One of them said, "Don't ask him to join us. He's so ugly." Little Green Caterpillar again ignored them and carried on eating. So he went on eating and eating until he became so tired and sleepy that he no longer cared to eat. He hunted for a warm bed in which to rest himself. He was so tired he could hardly crawl to the lowest branch of a bush. There he found a nice green leaf to wrap himself away from the cold wind, which started to blow. Little Green Caterpillar pulled his green blanket over his head but his toes were cold.

从前，有一只小绿毛虫，很快乐。他当然应该快乐啊！明媚的金色阳光洒在身上，花朵在微风的轻拂下优雅地点着头，鸟儿也在"啾啾"地唱着甜美的歌，最棒的是那舞动的小草，噢，太好吃了，因为小绿毛虫总是饥肠辘辘。

"你真丑陋，小绿毛虫，还特别懒惰，"蚂蚁路过时说，"整天躺在太阳底下无所事事！"小绿毛虫抬起头笑了笑，继续吃。

嗡嗡叫的蜜蜂从纺织工蜘蛛那儿听到一个消息，忍不住停下来告诉小绿毛虫他有多么丑陋。但是，小绿毛虫丝毫没有在意他的话，继续吃。

一群去参加舞会的蝴蝶经过，其中一个说："别让他加入我们，他太丑了。"小绿毛虫还是没在意他们，继续吃着。他吃啊吃啊，直到又累又困，再也不想吃了。他要去找一张暖床休息休息。他太累了，哪怕是最低的树枝也几乎爬不上去。开始刮风了，他找到一片完好的树叶，把自己裹起来免受寒风的侵袭。小绿毛虫拉过绿毯子盖住头顶时，脚却又受冻了。

"我一定要织一个壳来保暖。"小绿毛虫叹着气说，他开始觉得困了。于是，小绿毛虫开始织呀织。慢慢地，他的脚、甚至鼻子

❶ **caterpillar**
/'kætəpɪlə/
n. 毛虫
❷ **gracefully**
/'greɪsfulɪ/
adv. 优雅地

"I must spin a shell to keep me warm," sighed Little Green Caterpillar," as he was beginning to feel sleepy. So Little Green Caterpillar began to spin, and spin and spin. By-and-by, his toes and even his nose were covered with a pretty grey silken sheet. Little Green Caterpillar curled himself up in his cocoon[3] cradle and went to sleep. The world was lost to Little Green Caterpillar and who came and who went, he did not know.

Only when he heard the busy buzzing from Mr Bumble Bee, Little Green Caterpillar awoke. He saw the trees were covered with new green leaves. The cute young flowers had pushed their heads through the brown earth to swing in the sunshine.

"Oh dear, I must have slept for quite a while." Then Little Green Caterpillar crept out of his cocoon and found it was empty. "What happened to the Little Green Caterpillar?" he wondered. Along came a crowd of butterflies and they exclaimed, "Come on, brother, come and join us to the Biggest Butterfly Ball?" "Who am I?" he asked. "Don't you know you're one of us," the Chief Butterfly replied. Little did the Little Green Caterpillar realize that he had turned into a handsome Meadow[4] Brown Butterfly!

Who was the creator who turned the ugly Green Caterpillar into a handsome butterfly? Is it the work of nature? But whatever you think, the ugly Green Caterpillar had to sleep and wait its turn before it became a butterfly.

都被一层漂亮的灰色丝膜包住了。小绿毛虫
蜷缩在茧做的摇篮里入睡了。对小绿毛虫来
说，世界消失了，孰来孰往，他也不知道。

直到小绿毛虫听见蜜蜂繁忙的叫声时才
醒过来。他看见树木都长满了新叶子，可爱
的小花朵也从褐色的土壤中探出了头，在阳
光下摇摆着。

"噢，天哪，我肯定睡了好长时间。"小
绿毛虫从茧里爬出来，茧空了。"小绿毛虫
怎么啦？"他很纳闷。这时来了一群蝴蝶，
他们都喊着："来呀，哥们儿，来和我们一
起去参加最大的蝴蝶舞会吧。""我是谁
呀？"小绿毛虫问道。"你不知道吗？你是
我们中的一员啊，"蝴蝶首领答道。小绿毛
虫几乎没有意识到自己已经变成一只美丽的
褐色蝴蝶了。

是谁把丑陋的绿毛虫变成了一只美丽的
蝴蝶呢？是大自然的杰作吗？但是，不管你
怎样想，丑陋的绿毛虫都要等待时机才能变
成蝴蝶。

❸ cocoon
/kə'kuːn/
n. 茧
❹ meadow
/'medəu/
n. 草地

What friendship means to me?

友谊对我意味着什么？

But just knowing you has shaped my life more than you could ever think.

然而认识你就塑造了我的生活，而且远远超出你的想像。

I have a list of folks I know all written in a book, and every now and then I go and take a look. That is when I realize these names they're a part, not of the book they're written in but taken from the heart.

For each name stands for someone who has crossed my path sometime, and in that meeting they have become the reason and the rhyme. It may sound fantastic for me to make this claim, but I really am composed[1] of each remembered name. You may not be aware of any special link, but just knowing you has shaped my life more than you could ever think.

Please don't think my greeting as just a mere routine, your name was not forgotten in-between. For when I send a greeting that is addressed to you, it is because you're on the list of folks I'm indebted to[2]. So whether I've known you for many days or few, in some ways you have a part in shaping things I do. I total up the many folks I've met, you're a friend I would prefer never to forget.

我在一个本子里记下了很多朋友的名字，偶尔翻开瞧瞧时，我意识到这些名字不仅记在本子上，而且记在心灵深处。

　　每一个名字都代表着一个人，他们在特定时间进入我的生命轨迹，因为与他们相遇，我变得更加理智。我这样说可能听起来很不可思议，但是我实际是由我所记得的每一个名字共同塑造的。你可能意识不到这其中有丝毫特殊的联系，然而你的出现给我的生活带来重大影响，而且远远超出你的想像。

　　不要以为我的问候只是形式，你的名字在问候中不会被遗忘。我向你打招呼，是因为你是我要感激的一个人。所以不管我认识你很久，还是几天，在某种程度上你都影响了我的处事方式。想想我所遇到的人，你是我永远不能忘怀的一个朋友。

❶ compose
/kəm'pəʊz/
v. 组成
❷ be indebted to
感激

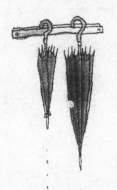

True Heaven

真正的天堂

Oh, you mean the place with golden street and pearly gates? Nope. That's Hell.

你说的那个地方是不是有金子铺的街道和珍珠做的门？不，那是地狱。

A man and his dog were walking along a road. The man was enjoying the scenery, when it suddenly occurred to him that he was dead. He remembered dying, and that the dog had been dead for years. He wondered where the road would lead them.

After awhile, they came to a high, white stone wall along one side of the road. It looked like fine marble.

At the top of a long hill, the wall was broken by a tall arch that glowed in the sunlight. As the man stood before it, he saw a magnificent[1] gate in the arch that looked like it was made of mother of pearl. The street that led to the gate looked like it was paved with pure gold.

He and the dog walked toward the gate, and as he got closer, he saw a man at a desk to one side. When he was close enough, he called out, "Excuse me, where are we? "

"This is Heaven, sir", the man answered.

"How! Would you happen to have some water? "

"Of course, sir. Come right in, and I'll have some ice water brought right up."

The man gestured, and the gate began to open.

"My friend come in too?" the traveler asked, gesturing to ward his dog.

一个人带着他的狗在路上边走边欣赏风景，突然，他想起来自己已经死了。他记得他死了，而且狗也死了几年了。他不知道这条路会把他们带到哪里。

过了一会儿，他们沿路来到一座高高的白石墙前，墙看起来像精美的大理石建的。

在一座绵延的小山顶上，墙体被一扇在阳光下闪闪发光的拱门断开了。这个人站在门前时，看见拱门里有一扇华丽的小门，门看起来就像是用珍珠贝制成的，通向小门的街道像是纯金铺成的。

他和狗朝这扇门走去，一直往里走时，他看见一旁的桌子边坐着一个人。走近时，他大声问："请问，这是什么地方？"

"这是天堂，先生。"那人回答。

"太棒啦！您这儿有水喝吗？"

"当然，先生。快进来吧，我马上给您准备些冰水来。"那人示意了一下，门开了。

"我的朋友也可以进来吗？"行人指着他的狗问道。

"很抱歉，我们不接待宠物。"

行人想了片刻，然后转身继续沿原路前行。

❶ magnificent
/mæɡˈnɪfɪsənt/
adj. 华丽的

"I'm sorry; sir, but we don't accept pets."

The traveler thought a moment and then turned back toward the road and continued the way he had been going.

After another long walk, and at the top of another long hill, he came to a dirt road which led through a farm gate that looked as if it had never been closed. There was no fence. As he approached the gate, he saw a man inside, leaning[2] against a tree and reading a book.

"Excuse me!" He called to the reader. "Do you have any water?"

"Yeah, sure, there's a pump[3] over there." The reader pointed to a place that couldn't be seen from outside the gate. "Come on in."

"How about my friend here?" the traveler gestured to his dog.

"There should be a bowl by the pump."

They went through the gate, and sure enough, there was an old-fashioned hand pump with a bowl beside it.

The traveler filled the bowl and took a long drink himself, then he gave some to his dog.

又走了很长一段路程之后，在另一座绵延的小山顶上，他走上一条通往一个农场大门的土路，农场的门好像从未关上过似的，也没有篱笆。他走到门口，看见里面有个人倚在树旁看书。

"打扰一下！"他对看书的人说，"能给点儿水喝吗？"

"当然，那边有个水泵。"看书的人朝一个地方指了指，但从门外看不见这个地方。"进来吧。"

"我的朋友可以进来吗？"行人指着他的狗问道。

"水泵旁边应该有一只碗。"

他们走进门来，果真看到有一台老式手摇水泵，旁边还有一只碗。

行人把碗里盛满水，自己喝了一大口，接着又给狗喝了点儿。

他们喝饱之后，转身走向站在树边等他们的那个人。

"这儿是什么地方？"行人问。

"这儿是天堂。"他回答。

"天哪，真搞不懂，"行人说，"沿这条路往下走，那里也有个人说他那儿是天堂。"

❷ lean
/liːn/
v. 斜靠着

❸ pump
/pʌmp/
n. 水泵

When they were full, he and the dog walked back toward the man who was standing by the tree waiting for them.

"What do you call this place?" the traveler asked.

"This is Heaven." was the answer.

"Hell, That's confusing[4]," the traveler said, "The man down the road said that was Heaven, too."

"Oh, you mean the place with golden street and pearly gates? Nope. That's Hell."

"Doesn't it make you mad they use the name Heaven like that?" "No. I can see how you might think so, but we're just happy that they screen out the folks who leave their best friends behind."

　　"你说的那个地方是不是有金子铺的街道和珍珠做的门？不，那是地狱。"

　　"他们和你们用同一个的名字，难道你不生气吗？" "是的，我很生气。你有这种想法，我可以理解，但是，我们很高兴他们把你这个不愿对最好的朋友弃之不顾的人拒之门外。"

❹ confusing
/kənˈfjuːzɪŋ/
adj. 令人困惑的

A sip that slips

贪杯使人堕落

When he woke up, the holy man realized what he had done.

圣人醒来之后，意识到了自己的所作所为。

There once lived a holy man who was renown for his piety. He had only a meal a day and was often found to be in a state of meditation[1] and prayer. People flocked to seek the holy man for advice. He administered each one according to his/her needs. Soon news spread that this holy man wanted to build a temple to train those interested in his teachings. One day he was called to the king's palace.

This was what the king said to him: "Holy Sir, I heard that you want to build a temple. You have my support but may I ask that you pass some simple test first. There are five rooms which you will have to pass through. In each room will be a question. Just answer each accordingly[2] and if all your answers are correct, you need only to retreat your steps and return the way you came. I will give you whatever sum you need to build the temple. "

The first room was empty and the holy man heard a voice.
"Have you ever lied?" .... *"No."*
Second room was filled with all kinds of swords.
"Have you ever killed?" .... *"No."*
Third room laid a beautiful woman with long black hair.
"Have you ever commit adultery[3]?" .... *"No."*
Fourth room was filled with various types of meat.
"Have you ever tasted meat?" ....*"No."*
Fifth was filled with different bottles of wine.
"Have you ever tasted alcoholic drinks?" ....*"No."*

从前，有一位以虔诚著称的圣人。他每天只吃一顿饭，而且经常有人看见他沉思、祈祷。人们云集而来，向圣人求教，圣人都会根据每个人的需要予以指点。不久，圣人要修建一座庙宇以便把他的思想传授给那些对他的学说感兴趣的人们，这个消息传开了。一天，他被召进了国王的王宫。

国王对他说了下边这些话："圣人先生，我听说你要建造一座庙宇。我很支持你，但是，我要求你先通过我的一个简单的测试。你要进入五个房间，每个房间里有一个问题。按要求回答每个问题，如果你都答对了，只需退出大殿，回去就是了。不论你建庙宇需要多少钱，我都会给你。"

第一个房间是空的，圣人听到有问话的声音。

你撒过谎吗？.................."没有。"

第二个房间里装满了各种各样的剑。

"你杀过人吗？".................."没有。"

第三个房间里躺着一个长发美女。

"你与人通奸过吗？"............"没有。"

第四个房间里是各种各样的肉。

"你吃过肉吗？".................."没有。"

第五个房间里是各种各样的酒。

"你喝过酒吗？".................."没有。"

❶ meditation
/ˌmedɪˈteɪʃən/
n. 思考
❷ accordingly
/əˈkɔːdɪŋlɪ/
adv. 按要求，照着
❸ adultery
/əˈdʌltərɪ/
n. 通奸

The holy man passed the tests. "What silly questions!" he thought to himself. He was about to leave the room when he spotted a tiny cup. He felt it would do him no harm if he just took a sip. So he poured some wine into the cup. As the wine caressed[4] his palate he took another sip and then another and was soon intoxicated[5]. Suddenly, he remembered that with wine he would enjoy himself more if he had some meat. With a small bite, his juices[6] multiplied and he longed for the beautiful woman with whom he could make merry. When he woke up, the holy man realized what he had done. He could not lie nor could he face the king. He took the sword and ended his life.

Moral: Beware of a little sip between the lips and the teeth!

圣人完成了测试。"多傻的问题啊!"他暗自想道。正当他要离开房间时,发现了一个小酒杯。他觉得只喝一小口对他不会有什么损害。因此,他往杯里倒了点儿酒。酒滋润了他的喉咙,他又喝了一口。就这样一口接一口,很快他就醉了。突然,他想起来喝酒时如果吃点儿肉会更加享受。吃了一小口肉之后,他精力大增,渴望与美女寻欢作乐。圣人醒来之后,意识到了自己的所作所为。他不能说谎,也无颜面对国王。他拿起剑结束了自己的生命。

寓意:警惕唇齿间的诱惑!

❹ **caress**
/kə'res/
v. 爱抚

❺ **intoxicated**
/ɪn'tɒksɪkeɪtɪd/
adj. 醉的

❻ **juice**
/dʒuːs/
n. 精力

An insignificant act of kindness

微不足道的善举

So he too pick up the starfishes and threw them into the sea.

于是,他也捡起海星,扔回大海。

A man was strolling[1] along the beach when he suddenly noticed from afar what he thought were children dancing. "What on
earth are they doing dancing on the beach?" as he quickly paced
towards them. He was surprised that a boy and a girl were not
dancing but picking up the starfishes which were washed ashore
by the tide and throwing them back into the sea.

"Excuse me, why are you throwing the starfishes back into
the sea?" he asked.

The children ignored[2] the remark but they continued picking
up the starfishes and kept throwing them back into the sea.

"Don't you think it is a waste of your time as there are hun-
dreds of starfishes still lying around. Surely you can't keep this
act all day long."

At last the elder boy replied, "Sir, you see the sun would soon
rise and the tide will ebb away. Though my sister and I can't throw
all the starfishes back into the sea, we are sure it matters to the
ones we succeed in throwing. Would you like to join us, it would
make a difference." The man smiled and said, "It certainly would,"
so he too pick up the starfishes and threw them into the sea.

Moral: A little drop of water can make a might ocean.

有一个人在沙滩上散步，突然，他看到远处好像是有孩子们在跳舞。"他们在沙滩上跳舞干什么呢？"他边想边迅速朝他们走过去。他惊奇地发现，一个男孩和一个女孩并不是在跳舞，而是在捡被海水冲上岸来的海星，把它们扔回大海。

"请问，你们为什么要把海星扔回大海呢？"他问。

孩子们没有理会他的话，继续捡海星扔回大海。

"你们不觉得这是浪费时间吗？还有成千上万只海星躺在岸上呢！你们肯定不会一整天都这样扔下去吧。"

终于，年龄大一点儿的男孩开口了，"先生，你知道，太阳很快就要升起来了，潮水也会退去。虽然我和妹妹不能把所有的海星都扔回大海，但我相信，对于被我们扔回大海的海星来说，我们所做的是至关重要的。你想加入我们吗？这很有意义。"那人笑了笑说："当然。"于是，他也捡起了海星，扔回大海。

寓意：一小滴水亦可汇成浩瀚的海洋。

❶ stroll
/strəul/
v. 散步
❷ ignore
/ɪɡˈnɔː/
v. 不理会

The lizard

蜥　蜴

How could the lizard survive in such a painful posture in the dark wall partition without moving?

蜥蜴怎么可能以这么痛苦的姿势一动不动地在黑暗的板墙夹缝中生存下来呢？

A Japanese owner wanted to renovate[1] his house. As most Japanese homes have a hollow space between the wooden walls, it was normal to tear open the walls first. The owner's young son, who was always trying to build something with his hands, told the father, "When I grow up I want to be an architect. Can I see what happens to the walls when they are torn down?" "Of course, son, but you have to be careful that they do not fall on you."

"Father," the boy cried excitedly, "I see a nail from outside had stuck into one of the lizard's feet on the wooden wall. It's still alive?" "How could that be," the father shouted. He remembered that the house was built ten years ago. How could the lizard survive in such a painful posture in the dark wall partition without moving? Both father and son were determined to find out how the lizard survived this ordeal all these years.

Work was temporarily[2] stopped and they observed the lizard. Surely someone must have been feeding it but who? Suddenly, from out of nowhere, another lizard appeared, with food in its mouth. The owner and his son were stunned to see the lizard with food in its mouth feeding the lizard stuck by the nail. The mystery was solved. They were so overwhelmed at what they saw.

The father slowly took out the nail from the lizard's feet and told his son, "We will nurse the lizard back to health. Shall we keep it as our house pet?" "Father, what about its kind saviour[3]?" So the two lizards were allowed to roam around the house freely without any disturbance[4].

一个日本房主想修葺自己的房子。因为大多数日式房子的木板隔墙之间都有空隙，所以，一般都先拆墙。这位房主的小儿子一直想自己动手建造点儿什么，就对父亲说："我长大了要做一名建筑师，我可不可以看看墙是怎样被拆开的？""当然，儿子，不过你要当心，别被墙砸着。"

"爸爸，"男孩兴奋地喊道，"我看见一个钉子从外面把一只蜥蜴的脚钉在了木板上。它还活着呢！""怎么可能呢？"父亲大声说。他记得这座房子是 10 年前建造的。蜥蜴怎么可能以这么痛苦的姿势一动不动地在黑暗的板墙夹缝中生存下来呢？父亲和儿子都决定要调查出这些年来蜥蜴是如何熬过这一苦难历程的。

他们暂时停下手中的活来观察蜥蜴。肯定有谁一直在喂养着蜥蜴，但是，会是谁呢？突然，不知从哪儿又跑来了一只蜥蜴，口里含着食物。当看到口里含着食物的蜥蜴给被钉子钉住的蜥蜴喂食时，房主和儿子都惊得目瞪口呆。迷团解开了。他们都被所见到的情形折服了。

父亲将钉子从蜥蜴的脚上慢慢拔出来，对儿子说："我们来照顾它，让它恢复健康吧。我们把它当作家里的宠物来养，好吗？"

❶ **renovate**
/ˈrenəʊveɪt/
v. 修葺

❷ **temporarily**
/ˈtempərərɪlɪ/
adv. 暂时地

❸ **savior**
/ˈseɪvjə/
n. 拯救者，恩人

❹ **disturbance**
/dɪsˈtɜːbəns/
n. 打扰

Moral: If this simple story had touched your heart, then tear away the wall of hatred, prejudice[5], jealousy, greed and replace it with love, care and share.

"爸爸，它那可爱的救命恩人怎么办呢？"最后，他们允许两只蜥蜴在家里随意走动，不受任何干扰。

　　寓意：如果这篇简短的故事触动了你的心灵，那么就请拆掉仇恨、偏见、嫉妒、贪婪之墙，代之以仁爱、关怀、分享吧！

❺ prejudice
/ˈpredʒʊdɪs/
n. 成见；偏见

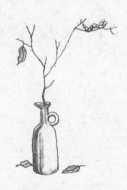

Don't be a frog in the well

不要做井底之蛙

Let me remain hidden in this well and no one cares whether I live or die.

就让我躲在这口井里吧，没有人会在乎我的死活。

There was once a frog who lived in a well. He was content and considered himself safe from the outside world. Actually this frog nicknamed The Leap was a hero in his village. The Leap won many feats[1] and for several years was champion during the Frog Leaping Contest. His leap was strong and long and he never lost a game. Soon The Leap boasted that no other frogs could beat him.

One day, a shy and timid frog appeared and said he would like to compete with The Leap. "My leap will be a mile long and I will crash you under my feet," The Leap boasted. That night before the event, The Leap dreamt that he was beaten by this insignificant timid competitor. He could not sleep and when morning came, his eyes were drowsy[2] but still he boasted that he would be unbeaten. On the last lap of the race over a wall, The Leap, closed his weary eyes and missed the target. He lost the race to the timid frog. The Leap was so ashamed that he ran away and fell into a well. At first he tried to leap out but failed. As time went on, he made no further attempts. "Let me remain hidden in this well and no one cares whether I live or die," he moaned pitifully.

One day, he heard loud croaking sound that came from outside the well. As he looked up, he saw the timid frog who had beaten him in the competition looking down at him. "What do you want and how did you find me?" The Leap shouted. "Have you come to humiliate[3] me, leave me alone." "Oh, no, replied the timid frog, "I was sent to look out for you and I went from one well

从前，有一只青蛙住在井里。他很满足，认为自己很安全，不会受到外界的伤害。事实上，这只绰号为"跳跃"的青蛙是村子里的英雄。"跳跃"创下了许多佳绩，有好几年都是蛙跳比赛的冠军。他跳得很远而且有力，在比赛中从未输过。不久，"跳跃"就吹嘘说没有青蛙能打败他。

有一天，来了一只胆小、害羞的青蛙，说他想与"跳跃"比试比试。"我能跳一英里远，而且能一脚把你踩得粉碎。""跳跃"吹嘘道。在比赛前的那天晚上，"跳跃"梦见自己被这个不起眼的、胆小的竞争对手打败了。他无法入睡，天亮以后，他睡眼惺忪，但还是吹嘘自己战无不胜。在跨墙比赛的最后阶段，"跳跃"闭上了疲惫的双眼，结果，未能跨过墙去。在这场比赛中，他输给了那只胆小的青蛙。"跳跃"羞愧难当，离家出走，掉进了一口井里。起初，他还想办法跳出来，但都失败了。时间久了，他就不再做这种尝试了。"就让我躲在这口井里吧，没有人会在乎我的死活。"他可怜地呻吟着说。

有一天，他听到从井外传来很响的蛙叫声。他抬起头一看，发现曾在比赛中击败他的那只胆小的青蛙正朝下看着他。"你想要

❶ feat
/fiːt/
n. 成绩
❷ drowsy
/ˈdrauzɪ/
adj. 昏昏欲睡的
❸ humiliate
/hjuːˈmɪlɪeɪt/
v. 羞辱

to another. Thank goodness I have found you at last. Our village
still needs you! There will be a competition with our neighboring
village and please try to leap out of the well and help us."

Suddenly, he saw his mother peering[4] down at him. "Son,
please come home. We never gave up looking for you," cried his
mother. "Please be careful, mother, or you will fall into the well,"
the Leap cried in return. After more encouraging words that he is
still much loved and unforgotten, The Leap made great efforts to
leap up from his hiding well onto the outside world. He was surprised to find his father and all his fellow frogs welcoming him
back to their fold.

"How long have I been in the well?" the Leap asked. "A year
or 365 days! " his father said. "Far too long," the other frogs
shouted. After The Leap got back his health, he had to train hard
to get into shape.

The competitive village sent their own hero frog and support-
ers to cheer their team. But The Leap proved that his leaping
skills were still as good as before. Both frogs had to leap over one
obstacle[5] or another. It was a hard fight but The Leap finally won
the race.

After the event was over, it was already arranged that the
next competition would be at their rival's village. But there was no
animosity[6] between the two groups. They were game enough to

干什么？你怎么找到我的？" "跳跃"喊道，"你是来羞辱我的吗？别烦我了。" "噢，不是，"胆小的青蛙答道，"我是被派来找你的，我一口井一口井地找，谢天谢地，总算找到你了。我们的村子还需要你啊！我们要和邻村比赛，请想办法跳出来帮我们吧。"

突然，他看见母亲也在朝下望着他，"儿子，回家吧。我们一直都在找你。"母亲哭着说。"小心点儿，妈妈，你会掉下来的。" "跳跃"也哭着说。在人们又说了些还很爱他、没有忘记他之类的鼓励话之后，"跳跃"竭尽全力从藏身之井跳了出来，回到了外面的世界。他惊讶地发现，他的父亲和伙伴们也都在欢迎他回到他们中间。

"我在井里待了多长时间？" "跳跃"问。"一年，365天！"他父亲说。"太长了。"其他青蛙喊道。等身体恢复之后，"跳跃"要刻苦训练以恢复身体素质。

比赛时，邻村派出了自己的英雄青蛙，还派出了支持者给他们呐喊助威。但是，"跳跃"证明了自己的跳跃能力依然像以前一样棒。两只青蛙都要跳过一道道障碍物。这是一场硬战，但是，"跳跃"最后赢得了比赛。

这次赛事结束后，下一场比赛被安排在

❹ peer
/pɪə/
v. 看
❺ obstacle
/ˈɒbstəkl/
n. 障碍物
❻ animosity
/ˌænɪˈmɒsɪtɪ/
n. 仇恨

admit that The Leap was the best so he won the race!

The Leap was asked to make a speech and this was his advice, "I was a frog in the well for a year and if not for your support, I might still be there. Of course, it hurts to lose but in any competition, there is a winner and a loser. Just try and try again and do your best the next time." The Leap promised to train the young frogs in the art of leaping but they must be prepared to work hard at it.

While celebrating the happy occasion and cheering The Leap, all his fellow frogs sang this song: "For he's our jolly good hero... and so says all of us..."

Moral: Don't sit on your laurels[7] as there's always someone who may be better than you!

对手的村里举行。但是，两队之间并没有仇恨。比赛足以证明"跳跃"是最棒的，所以他赢了比赛。

"跳跃"被要求做一次演讲，他提出了如下的建议："我是一只在井里待了一年的青蛙，如果没有你们的支持，我可能还在那里待着。当然，输掉比赛会令人痛心；但任何比赛都有输赢。只要努力，再努力，下一次竭尽全力就够了。""跳跃"答应帮助年轻青蛙训练跳跃技巧，但是，他们必须做好苦练的准备。

当庆祝这一快乐时刻，为"跳跃"喝彩时，他所有的伙伴都唱起了这首歌，"他是我们的大英雄，我们大家都这样认为……"

寓意：不要自满，因为总会有人胜过你！

❼ laurel
/ˈlɒrəl/
n. 桂冠

The silver ring

银戒指

Lizzie kept the ring carefully but she was reluctant to open it.

丽兹一直小心保存着戒指，但她却不愿打开它。

Lizzie stood by her father's bedside. He was suffering from cancer for many years. "Don't cry, Lizzie," he told her. "When the time comes and I shall no longer be with you, I want you to promise me that you'll not be sad." He also told her that she would be well taken care of. "I've a gift for you, darling Lizzie. It's our family heirloom. With it go three wishes."

"It's a beautiful silver ring," exclaimed Lizzie.

"You'll see cut on the inside are three circles. Whenever you're sad, open it up and you'll remember what I am going to tell you.

"The first is that your mind may be like a river, the second is that your whole life may be like the flowers and the third that your body may grow strong like the oak tree."

The father died shortly after. As the years passed by, Lizzie kept the ring carefully but she was reluctant[1] to open it. She loved to spend her school vacation at her grandma's country house by the sea. Her grandma loved her garden, which was surrounded with beautiful flowers and a tall oak tree.

"Lizzie," her grandma used to say, "this oak tree was planted by your grandpa when he was a little boy. Your father loved this tree and used to climb it. See how strong it still stands."

When her grandma died, Lizzie inherited[2] the country house.

丽兹站在父亲的床边，他患癌症已有多年了。"不要哭，丽兹，"父亲对她说，"死神来临的时候，我不能再陪在你身边了，我要你答应我不会难过。"他还说，她会得到很好的照顾的。"我有件礼物给你，亲爱的丽兹。这是我们家的传家之宝，它蕴涵着三个愿望。"

"这是一只漂亮的银戒指。"丽兹称赞道。

"你会看到内侧刻着三个圆圈。每当你难过的时候，就打开它，你会想起我现在要对你说的话。

"第一个愿望是愿你的思想如河流，第二个愿望是愿你的整个人生如花朵，第三个愿望是愿你的身体如橡树般强壮。"

说完不久，父亲去世了，时光一年一年逝去，丽兹一直小心保存着戒指，却不愿打开它。学校放假时，她喜欢待在祖母的海边农场里。祖母很喜欢自己的花园，花园四周开满了美丽的鲜花，还有一棵高大的橡树。

"丽兹，"祖母常说，"这棵橡树是你祖父小时候种的。你父亲非常喜欢这棵树，经常爬到树上玩。你看它现在依然还是那么强壮。"

祖母去世后，丽兹继承了农场。她在整

❶ reluctant
/rɪˈlʌktənt/
adj. 不情愿的

❷ inherit
/ɪnˈherɪt/
v. 继承

She was cleaning up her grandma's cupboard when she read a note addressed to her.

My dear granddaughter Lizzie,

Why are you afraid to open the silver ring your father left you? Life is full of surprises and I'm sure he is waiting for you to fulfill your promise. Don't linger any longer. Go for it and open the ring! I too will be watching over you.

Your loving grandma.

One bright morning, Lizzie decided to put the ring on her finger and trotted[3] off for a walk in the woods. On the way, she passed over a bridge that crossed the river.

She stopped to look down at the river, and as the little wavelets splashed together gently, Lizzie stood still, as if she heard the wavelets whispering to her:

"Don't you see that the stream never cease to move onward?"

"Yes, I know but why do you tell me that?" Lizzie answered.

"Don't you see, that is why your father wants your mind to be like a river. If it stayed still it would become stagnant[4]."

Lizzie then fluttered through the flowers. She bent down to smell them and she heard the flowers singing to her.

理祖母的衣橱时突然发现了祖母留给她的一
张便条。

亲爱的孙女丽兹：

　　你为什么不敢打开你父亲留给你的戒指
呢？生活中处处都有意想不到的事，我相信
他一直在等你实现自己的诺言。别再犹豫
了，去把戒指打开吧！我也会一直守护着你
的。

　　　　　　　　　　　　爱你的祖母

　　一个晴朗的早晨，丽兹决定把戒指戴在
手上，到树林里去散步。半路上，她经过一
座横跨小河的桥。

　　她停下来朝河里望去，细小的水波互相
轻柔地拍打着。丽兹一动不动地站在那儿，
好像她听到了水波在对她轻声耳语：

　　"难道你没有看到河水永不停息地奔向
前方吗？"

　　"我知道，但你为什么告诉我这些呢？"
丽兹回答。

　　"你不知道吗？这就是你父亲希望你的
思想如河流的原因。如果河水停滞不前，就
会变得腐臭。"

　　后来，丽兹在花丛中欢快地穿梭。她弯
腰去闻花香，听到花儿对她歌唱。

　　"我们很美丽，我们很美丽。"

❸ **trot**
/trɒt/
v. 散步
❹ **stagnant**
/ˈstægnənt/
adj. 腐臭的

"We are beautiful, we are beautiful."

"Yes you are indeed beautiful but why do you tell me that? " Lizzie answered.

"Don't you see your father wants your whole life to be beautiful."

Lizzie could not contain herself and fled away when she came to the oak tree. She climbed the tree and clung to its branches, while the leaves clustered[5] around her and she heard them say:

"An oak tree grows upright and is very strong."

"I know but what do you tell me that," Lizzie answered for the third time.

"Don't you see that is what your father wants your body to be strong as an oak tree."

At last, Lizzie understood the meaning of the three circles cut inside the silver ring and the three wishes that go with it. She never took off the ring from her finger. Whenever she saw the three · circles, she tried to make the wishes come true, thus fulfilling her promise to her father.

Moral: A dream is still a dream until you act upon it.

"是的，你们的确很美丽，但你们为什么要告诉我这些呢？"丽兹问。

"你不知道你父亲希望你的整个人生都很美丽吗？"

丽兹不能自已，跑开了。她来到橡树旁，爬上树，攀在树干上。树叶簇拥着她，她听到它们说：

"橡树长得挺拔而强壮。"

"我知道，但你们为什么告诉我这些呢？"丽兹第三次回答。

"你不知道吗？你父亲就是希望你的身体如橡树般强壮啊。"

最后，丽兹终于明白了刻在戒指内侧的三个圆圈和戒指所蕴涵的三个愿望。她再也没有把戒指从手上摘下来。每当看到这三个圆圈，她总会努力去实现那三个愿望，也实现她对父亲许下的诺言。

寓意：若不付诸行动，梦想将永远只是梦想。

⑤ cluster
/ˈklʌstə/
v. 簇拥

The royal road to greatness

通向伟大的坦途

*Bid him return, for this man truly has 'greatness'
within him.*

让他回来吧，因为这个人身上具有真正
的"伟大"。

A king once lived in a palace, which stood where all roads of the world met. He was indeed the most-powerful man on the planet. But he was also a kind and wise king. He would not turn anyone away and he built a house where travelers could rest and food provided.

One day, three strangers appeared before the palace door. They had traveled a long way to meet him. After they had rested and had their stomachs filled, they were ushered[1] into the king's room.

One of the spokesman among them said, "Your Majesty, we are three brothers and we have traveled a long way as we heard much about your power. If you could grant us 'greatest' our search would be over. Then we would understand what 'greatest' means.

The king replied, "Yes, I am great but I cannot bestow[2] 'greatness' upon any man. The most I am permitted is to point the pathway along which 'greatness' may be found."

The three brothers were told a path each had to take. Six servants were to help them to achieve their "greatness." A messenger who would also accompany him would observe what each man did and then report to the king.

For days they traveled along the roads, looking eagerly for "greatness." At last the brothers came to a huge mountain that rose like a great rock almost touching the big blue sky above.

从前，处于世界上所有道路交汇之处的一座宫殿里住着一个国王。他是地球上最强大的人，但他也是一个和善英明的国王。他不会把任何人拒之门外，他还修建了一座房屋，为行人提供食宿。

有一天，三个陌生人出现在宫殿门口。他们经过了长途跋涉来见国王，休息片刻并填饱肚子之后，他们被带到了国王的房间。

他们之中的一位代表说："陛下，我们是三兄弟，听过许多关于您的能力超群的故事，所以我们长途跋涉来到这里。如果您能赐予我们'伟大'，我们的寻访就可以结束了。到那时侯，我们就会明白'伟大'的含义了。"

国王回答："对，我是伟大的，但我不能把'伟大'赠予任何人。我能够做的最多也就是指出可能找到'伟大'的道路。"

国王指给三兄弟一条路，每个人都要走，将有六名仆人帮助他们获得"伟大"。一名陪同的信使将观察每个人的所作所为，并报告给国王。

他们沿路走了几天，热切地寻找着"伟大"。终于，三兄弟来到了一座大山前，大山像一块巨石一样耸立着，直冲云霄。当他们见到这座大山时，都惊呆了。大致看了一

❶ usher
/ˈʌʃə/
v. 带领

❷ bestow
/biˈstəu/
v. 赠予

They were dismayed[3] when they saw this mountain but after they scanned the heights they realized it was the thing they had sought.

"Alright, this must be the path we must take to 'greatness'," they cried out eagerly.

The first brother called out to the six servants and said, "Carry as many stones as you can and make steps that I may ascend." When every stone was put in place, they came short of the mountaintop. He was angry and commanded that with their bodies; the six servants should complete the steps. Then over their bodies and over their shoulders, the man climbed but he still could not reach the mountaintop. He was only an arm's length to his "greatness" prize.

The messenger returned and reported to the king what he saw. "A most strange figure to behold[4]. He could not reach the top nor climb down. As I am now speaking, Your Majesty, the man would perhaps still be standing like a rock with his arm upstretched."

The second brother called out to the servants and the messenger. "I have found a pathway where there is only one room for me. You all return to the king lest you impede[5] my progress," as he dismissed them away.

When the king heard what had happened, he was sad, and sent other servants to seek the man should he needed help. They

下山的高度之后他们意识到，这就是他们寻找的东西。

"好啦，这一定就是我们必须走的通向'伟大'的路。"他们急切地说道。

老大对六名仆人大声说："尽可能多搬些石头来搭台阶让我上去。"他们把石头放好沿着爬上去，但最后离山顶还有一段距离。他非常生气，下令六名仆人用他们的身体补齐台阶。后来，这个人爬过他们的身体和肩膀，但是依然够不到山顶。他距离他的"伟大"只有一臂之遥。

信使回来，将他所见到的报告给了国王。"那样子看起来非常奇怪。他够不到山顶，也下不来。现在我说话的时候，陛下，那个人可能还像岩石一样站在那里，伸着胳膊往上够呢。"

老二对仆人和信使大声说："我已经找到了一条路，那里只能我一个人走。你们都回到国王那里去吧，免得妨碍我的进程。"他一边说着一边把他们打发走了。

国王听到所发生的事很难过，他又派了其他仆人去看这个人是否需要什么帮助。他们在蜿蜒的小路上发现了这个人的足迹，却哪儿都找不到他。他永远也不会到达山顶了。

③ **dismayed**
/dɪsˈmeɪd/
adj. 惊呆的
④ **behold**
/bɪˈhəʊld/
v. 看，观察
⑤ **impede**
/ɪmˈpiːd/
v. 阻碍，妨碍

found his footprints on the winding path but the man was nowhere to be found, and he never reached the top.

The third brother said to the servants, "You all remain below, I will make use of my hand and foot and slowly climb to the top. When he had gone a little way up, he looked down and saw the servants watching admiringly at what he was doing. He shouted as loud as he could and asked, "would you all like to join me?" And from the echo of the wind, he heard, "Yes, we would love to come up with you." The man descended[6] and with bended shoulders helped each one of them up the rock. "Together we will succeed! " he exclaimed.

The messenger told the king what this man had done. "Bid him return, for this man truly has 'greatness' within him."

Moral: United we stand, divided we fall.

老三对仆人说："你们都待在下面，我会用我的手和脚慢慢爬上山顶的。"他往上爬了一段之后，朝下看了看，发现仆人们都在羡慕地望着他。他使劲喊道："你们想和我一起上去吗？"他听到了风传来的回音："是的，我们想和你一起上去。"这个人下来了，他们弯下腰，互相帮扶着朝山顶爬去。"大家一起努力，我们会成功的！"他呼喊着。

信使把这个人的所作所为告诉了国王。"让他回来吧，因为这个人身上具有真正的'伟大'。"

寓意：团结可制胜，分散必败亡。

❻ descend
/dɪˈsend/
v. 下来

The crafty old cat

狡猾的老猫

All his friends had fled away and he was alone, with no one to care for him.

他所有的朋友都跑了，只剩下他自己，没有一个人关心他。

The mice were having a jolly good time. The barns of the old farmhouse were full of grain. In the mornings the mice would nowhere to be seen. They hid among the stacks of wheat or rice or in the tiny holes and crevices[1] around the farm so as not to draw attention.

Mr. Cat who had been around the barns knew the mice schedule. At nights they would come out to play and enjoy the night breeze. Their worst enemy, Mr. Cat, had changed into a new leaf. This means, seldom, if ever, would Mr. Cat hurt them now.

"How kind and friendly Mr. Cat has become！" said the mice.

Mr. Cat was a tricky one. He was getting old and rather weak and he did not like going without his "mice" for dinner. He used to have extra helping and could catch two or more mice a night but he felt his catching power was weakened. So he formed a plan, which he wanted to put into action. He had to win the confidence of the mice by playing with them fairly and squarely. Once he caught a baby mouse but he went to its mother and said, "Your dear little one must have strayed[2] from your bosom, my friend." The mother mouse was thankful for his kind deed.

As time went on, the mice poured their thoughts to Mr. Cat and even had him looked after the family if one father or mother mouse had to go somewhere. "You don't worry, friend, your babies will be safe with me," Mr. Cat said.

老鼠们过着快活的日子。古老农场的谷仓里堆满了谷物。早上根本看不见老鼠，为了不引起注意，他们藏在一堆堆的小麦或大米中，或藏在农场里各处的小洞或缝隙里。

猫先生在谷仓的四周巡视过，他很清楚老鼠的活动安排。他们会在夜里出来玩耍，享受晚风。他们的天敌猫先生已经改过自新了。也就是说，现在，猫先生即使会伤害他们，这种情况也很少了。

"猫先生变得多善良、多友好啊！"老鼠们说。

猫先生很有心计。他日渐年迈，身体虚弱，他可不喜欢没有老鼠的晚餐。过去他常常加餐，一晚上能抓两只或更多的老鼠，不过，他渐渐感觉到自己的捕捉能力下降了，所以，他想出了一个计划，并要把计划付诸实施。他必须赢得老鼠们的信任，于是让他们毫无戒备地和他玩儿。有一次，他逮住了一只小老鼠，但是他走到鼠妈妈跟前说："你的小宝宝一定是从你怀里跑出来迷路了，我的朋友。"鼠妈妈非常感激他的善举。

渐渐地，老鼠们都把自己的想法对猫先生和盘托出，甚至鼠爸爸或鼠妈妈要出门时，还托他照顾家人。"别担心，朋友，你的孩子们在我这儿很安全。"猫先生说。

❶ crevice
/ˈkrevɪs/
n. 缝隙
❷ stray
/streɪ/
v. 走失，迷路

Then one night, Mr. Cat called all his friends, the mice, and said, "I have a proposal to make. With age comes wisdom. I would like you to know that you've forgiven me for my past cruel deeds to you in my wild and thoughtless youth. From this day forward, you shall go where you like about the barns without any fear of attack from me. I will be a father to you, and watch over you and protect you. But there is only one condition I have to ask. You must acknowledge[3] me as your king and march before me in procession every night as I would like to see and know all your dear faces. "

One little squeaky voice cried out, "why must we march and not just sit around you? You could have a role call and identify us, one by one."

Mr. Cat, replied, "My dear friends, don't you think it would be lovely to march in a possession with the candle light shining around us as you all sing along. It would lit up your hearts and mine like one big happy family! "

"Indeed, this is the wisest plan I heard," a mother mouse said, "Mr. Cat once returned my little baby who had strayed away from me. He had already shown his true sincere color."

There were great cheers and all mice agreed to perform the nightly procession and bow to Mr. Cat, their king. As the procession passed before Mr. Cat, unknown to the mice when the last mouse was bowing, Mr. Cat quickly seized it tightly in his claws and killed it before it could give the tiniest shriek[4]. At other nights he managed

后来，有一天晚上，猫先生把他的老鼠朋友们叫了起来，对他们说："我有个提议。天增岁月人增智。我要告诉你们，你们已经宽恕了我过去的野蛮、卤莽和年轻时对你们的残忍行为，所以从今天起，你们可以去谷仓周围任何你们想去的地方，不用担心我抓你们了。我会做你们的父亲，照顾你们，保护你们。但是，我只有一个条件。你们必须承认我是你们的国王，每天晚上在我面前列队前进，因为我想看到你们，认识你们每一张可爱的面孔。"

一只嗓门尖细的小老鼠喊道："为什么我们必须列队前进，而不坐在你身边呢？你可以点名，一个一个地认识我们嘛。"

猫先生回答说："亲爱的朋友，你不觉得你们列队前进唱歌，再在我们周围点上蜡烛，这样更温馨吗？它会照亮你我的心房，我们就像一个大家庭！"

"这的确是我听过的最英明的计划，"一只鼠妈妈说，"猫先生曾把我走散的小宝宝还给了我，他已经展示了他诚挚的真面目。"

老鼠们欢天喜地，都同意晚上列队前进，向猫先生——他们的国王鞠躬行礼。前进的队伍经过猫先生时，他趁老鼠们不注意，迅速抓住最后一只向他鞠躬的老鼠，把

❸ acknowledge
/əkˈnɒlɪdʒ/
v. 承认
❹ shriek
/ʃriːk/
n. 尖叫

to seize two or more mice.

The number of mice was so great that even mice from other barns were invited when, by word of mouth, they heard about the procession. No one noticed the disappearance of any of his or her members.

There were, however, two mice that gradually became suspicious of their ruler. One was called Nini and the other Bibi. They were, in fact, husband and wife, and one of their little ones had been lost in the procession and had disappeared. Nini and Bibi discussed the matter and said this was what each should do during the procession.

While the procession was winding past Mr. Cat, Nini kept crying out in her shrill, shrieky voice, "Are you there, Bibi? Are you there Bibi?" And Bibi shouted in reply, "I'm coming, Nini, I'm coming! "

The nearer Nini approached to where Mr. Cat stood, the louder and more often did he call to his wife. "Are you there, Bibi?" Mr. Cat realized that if he pounced[5] on the last member of the procession all the mice would surely know of it. So he went hungry that night. But he felt sure that it was merely by accident Nini and Bibi had been first and last in line and he resolved to make up the next night by eating two mice. Much to his anger he found that Nini still headed the procession while Bibi stood at the rear. As soon as Nini started her cry, "Are you there Bibi? Are you there, Bibi?"

他紧紧抓在手里，还没等他叫出声来就把他掐死了。有的时候，他一晚上抓两只或更多。

老鼠的数量非常大，甚至当其他谷仓的老鼠听说列队前进之后也被邀请了来，没有人注意到队伍有什么损失。

然而，有两只老鼠渐渐开始怀疑他们的国王了。一只叫尼尼，另一只叫比比，事实上，他们是一对夫妻。他们的一个孩子在列队前进时不见了，尼尼和比比讨论了这件事，说每个人在列队前进时应该要警惕。

队伍蜿蜒前进经过猫先生时，尼尼用他那尖嗓门喊："比比，你在那儿吗？比比，你在那儿吗？"比比大声回答："我来啦，尼尼，我来啦！"

尼尼越接近猫先生所站的地方，他喊妻子的声音就越大，次数也越多。"你在那儿吗，比比？"猫先生意识到如果他突袭队尾的那只老鼠，所有的老鼠肯定都会知道的。所以，那天晚上他饿肚子了。但是，他觉得尼尼和比比肯定是碰巧在队首和队尾的，决定第二天晚上吃两只老鼠作为补偿。令他非常气愤的是，他发现依然是尼尼在队首，比比在队尾。尼尼一开始喊："你在那儿吗，比比？你在那儿吗？"比比就大声回答："我

⑤ pounce
/paʊns/
v. 突袭

Bibi answered in a loud voice, "I am coming, Nini, I am coming!"

Down pounced the disappointed Mr Cat into the middle of the procession. But, as all the mice had been warned beforehand, they scattered with remarkable speed and Mr Cat was left hungry in the empty barn. All his friends had fled away and he was alone, with no one to care for him. Even if he had left for other pastures, he would be too old to do much harm to the other mice.

Moral: We can fool someone once, twice but never thrice[6]!

来啦，尼尼，我来啦!"

失望的猫先生扑向了队伍的中间。但是，所有老鼠都被事先提醒过，飞快地散开了，只有猫先生一个人饿着肚子待在空荡荡的谷仓里。他所有的朋友都跑了，只剩下他自己，没有一个人关心他。即使他离开这里去别的农场，也已是老态龙钟，不会对其他老鼠造成什么伤害了。

寓意：愚人不过三!

❻ thrice
/θraɪs/
adv. 三次

The greatest gift of all

最好的礼物

"We are grateful for even the smallest offering," the man at the counter replied kindly.

"即使是最少的捐赠，我们也非常感激。"柜台旁负责的人和善地说。

At one stopover in a big town, a huge banner was written in bold letters: FAMINE IN AFRICA. PLEASE GIVE GENEROUSLY TO SAVE THE STARVING PEOPLE. A large crowd was queuing to hand over their donations[1].

Near the door of the town hall stood a beautiful young girl, poorly but neatly dressed. With shy glances she watched the people before her. She saw a merchant who laid a bag of gold on the table. Then came a rich lady with haughty[2] looks who offered a variety of jewels; some others handed cash, clothing's and foodstuff.

The girl was reluctant to take her turn but at last, summoning[3] up her courage, she stepped forward. "But...it is so small I am ashamed to offer it. It seems worthless, but it is all I have," she said. "We are grateful for even the smallest offering," the man at the counter replied kindly. "Here it is, I have nothing else to give," she added timidly. She drew under her cloak two long thick plaits of her golden hair. As she did so, the hood of her cloak fell back, showing the beautifully young head shorn of[4] its golden glory.

The generosity of this beautiful girl to donate her most priceless possession, her golden locks of hair, overshadowed all the glittering gold or jewels of the other donors.

在一个大镇上的中转站，挂着一条巨型横幅，上面用黑体字写着："非洲饥荒。请您慷慨解囊，拯救饥饿的人们。"在那儿有一大群人在排队捐赠。

市政厅的门旁站着一个漂亮的小姑娘，她的衣服的质地虽然很差，却很整洁。她注视着眼前的人们，眼里闪烁着害羞的神情。她看见一位商人把一袋金子放在了桌上，接着，一位傲慢的贵夫人拿出了各种珠宝，其他人也递上了现金、衣服和食物。

女孩还有犹豫要不要捐，最终她还是鼓起勇气走上前去。"可是……这太少了，我都不好意思拿出来。它看起来一文不值，但这是我所有的东西了。"她说道。"即使是最少的捐赠，我们也非常感激。"柜台旁负责的人和善地说。"给，我没有别的可捐了。"她羞怯地补充说。她从披风下拽出两根又长又粗的金色辫子。这时，披风的风帽掉了下来，露出已失去金色光环的漂亮的小脑袋。

这个漂亮的小姑娘慷慨地捐出了她最珍贵的财产——她的金发，令其他闪闪发光的金子、珠宝等捐赠物都黯然失色。

❶ **donation**
/dəʊˈneɪʃn/
n. 捐赠物
❷ **haughty**
/ˈhɔːtɪ/
adj. 傲慢的
❸ **summon**
/ˈsʌmən/
v. 鼓起
❹ **shorn of**
v. 失去…的

The lonely old man
孤独的老人

Well, I am not ashamed to say that I am passed eight times eight moons but I never met anyone I could call a friend for long.

活了 64 岁却没有遇到一个可以长久做朋友的人，我并不感到羞于启齿。

He was a little, wrinkled[1], all skin and bones, old man and lived all alone. No one knew much about him. One day he got a bad cold and he called for a doctor.

While the doctor was examining the old man, he asked, "Haven't you a friend who could come in to look after you?" "No, I have no friends — never had any", the old man replied. "What! You've lived in this village all your life and never had a friend! " "Well, I am not ashamed to say that I am passed eight times eight moons but I never met anyone I could call a friend for long. If it isn't one thing wrong with them, it's another." "Come, come! Our village headman, Mr Li, will surely come to your aid if he knows you are sick. I am sure you too know him." "Of course, I know him," replied the old man, "but he is such a bore. To hear him talk, you'd imagine the world had nothing in it but his wheat field and how wonderful and healthy his pigs are."

"Then what about Mr Ma who lives down the road?" "A more selfish fellow I ever came across, though I admit he has got a head on him. He has traveled and read many books and he's mighty[2] interesting to talk to. He used to come in here a lot at one time. But he would come only when he felt like doing so and he would stay away for long periods of time. I don't call that neighborly."

The doctor laughed. "You can't bring up anything against Mr Zhou? Everyone loves him." "You're right," agreed the old man. "Zhou would live on my doorstep if I let him. He's a bit of a wit

他是一个小老头，皮肤皱缩，瘦得皮包骨头，自己一个人住。大家对他都不太了解。有一天，他得了重感冒，便请来了一位医生。

医生给老人检查时问："你没有朋友来照顾你吗？""没有，我没有朋友——从来都没有。"老人回答。"什么！你在村子里住了一辈子，竟然连一个朋友也没有！""活了64岁却没有遇到一个可以长久做朋友的人，我并不感到羞于启齿。他们不是这方面不好，就是那方面有问题。""好啦，好啦！如果我们的村长李先生知道你病了，肯定会来帮你的。你肯定认识他吧。""当然，我认识他，"老人回答，"但是，他这个人很无聊，听他说话，你会觉得世界上就只有他的麦田和他那壮实、健康的猪。"

"那么住在这条街上马先生怎么样呢？""我从没见过这么自私的家伙，尽管我承认他有点儿头脑。他出去旅行过，读过很多书，和他聊天非常有趣。有一段时间，他常来我这里。但是，他只有在想来的时候才来，而且他会一连好长时间都不露面。我可不认为他这样做像个邻居的样。"

医生笑了。"你总不能挑出周先生的毛病吧？每个人都喜欢他。""你说的对，"老人表示同意，"如果我愿意，周先生会与我

❶ wrinkled
/ˈrɪŋkld/
adj. 皮肤皱缩的

❷ mighty
/ˈmaɪtɪ/
adv. 极，非常

and rattling[3] good company, but his noisy tongue makes my poor head ache."

"I'm afraid you see so much of your neighbor's failings[4] that you're blind to their virtues. You're a hard nut to crack, old man! Anyway, please call me if you need me. As a doctor I will attend to you regardless whether you like me or not!" the doctor re-marked as he took up his bag and hat to leave. The door banged and not a word of "thank you" was heard.

Moral: Be less mindful of other people's faults; try examining your own first!

住得很近。他很风趣，是个绝好的伴儿，但他说起话来吵得我头疼。"

"恐怕是你太看重邻居们的缺点而无视他们的优点了。老先生，您可真难伺候！不管怎样，需要的时候就叫我。作为一名医生，不管你喜不喜欢我，我都会照顾你的！"医生边说边拿起帽子离开了。门"嘭"的一声在身后关上了，医生连一句"谢谢"都没有听到。

寓意：别太在意他人的缺点；先自省一下！

❸ rattling
/ˈrætlɪŋ/
adv. 非常

❹ failing
/ˈfeɪlɪŋ/
n. 缺点，失败

The wise son

聪明的儿子

A brilliant bright radiance filled up the whole room.

明亮的烛光充满了整个房间。

A rich landowner who was well known for his wealth decided to leave his possession to his two sons. As he lay on his deathbed, he called the lads to him; at the break of dawn and even before the cock could crow. He then said, "I will leave all my wealth to the one who can best fill this room. It was in this room that I made plans on how to build up my fortune. Not an inch must be left uncovered. As I am getting weaker by the hour you both must come back by the stroke[1] of midnight, not a minute late. He handed each son a small piece of sliver and an empty gunny-sack[2] to put in their purchases.

They both went out and hurriedly came back with their purchases.

The eldest who had brought straw proceeded to spread it about the floor, but far from filling the room, it did not even cover half the space. "This is no use, son," said the father, "and let me see how your brother fills the room."

The younger son took from his bag a large candle and, setting it on table in the center of the room, lighted it. A brilliant bright radiance filled up the whole room. The father was delighted and exclaimed, "Son, you're worthy to be my successor[3] and I am sure you will use the wealth well."

一个以财富而闻名的地主决定将自己的财产留给两个儿子。临终前，他把孩子们叫到跟前；天刚蒙蒙亮，雄鸡尚未报晓。他说："你们谁能更好地把这间屋子装满，一寸也不能空着，我就把所有的财产留给谁。我就是在这间屋子里制定出如何积累财富的计划的。我就快不行了，你们必须在午夜的钟声敲响之前回来，一分钟也不能迟到。"他给了每个儿子一点儿银子和一个盛放货物的空麻袋。

两个儿子出去了，又带着货物急匆匆回来了。

大儿子买来了稻草，开始将稻草铺在地板上，但是，别说铺满整个屋子了，连一半也没有盖过来。"这没有用的，儿子，"父亲说。"让我看看你弟弟怎样装满这间屋子吧。"

小儿子从包里拿出一根大蜡烛，把它固定在屋子正中间的桌上点着了。明亮的烛光充满了整个房间。父亲高兴地称赞道："儿子，你应该成为我的继承人，我相信你会好好利用这笔财富的。"

❶ **stroke**
/strəʊk/
n. 敲钟声
❷ **gunnysack**
/ˈɡʌnɪsæk/
n. 麻袋
❸ **successor**
/səkˈsesə/
n. 继承人

The elaphant who never forgets
好记性的大象

The elephant bore the indignities with apparent indifference.

大象忍受着侮辱，装出满不在乎的样子。

A senseless[1] tailor, who frequently had occasion to pass a garden where an elephant was kept, took a cruel delight in teasing[2] the helpless creature. Each time he passed by the elephant he would play some dirty tricks. One day, he would prod[3] the elephant with a stick; another time he would hold out tempting[4] bits of food, and when the elephant reached out for the food, he would quickly withdraw his hand. He then roared with laughter.

The elephant bore the indignities with apparent indifference. There was no way the animal could hit the tailor back as his legs were chained and the garden gates locked.

But one day as the elephant was being led past the tailor's shop by its owner, it saw the tailor curled up on a low table. The man was heard snoring loudly and did not see the elephant. There was a wayside stream next to the tailor's shop. The elephant drew a quantity of water into its trunk and shot it full into the face of his sleeping enemy.

The tailor woke up with a fright to find not only his clothes were wet but his shop too. He was about to pick up a stick to hit the elephant when a crowd appeared. A young boy came out from among the crowd and said to the owner of the elephant, "Sir, I have seen with my own eyes how badly the tailor had treated the elephant! "

有个无聊的裁缝，每当他路过一个花园时，总要逗弄关在里面的无助的大象，从大象的痛苦中取乐。他每次经过大象时都要耍点儿鬼把戏。今天用棍子捅捅大象，明天又拿点儿诱人的食物来。当大象伸着鼻子够食物时，他就迅速把手抽回来，然后放声大笑。

大象忍受着侮辱，装出满不在乎的样子。它不能回击裁缝，因为它的腿上绑着链子，花园的门也锁着。

但是，有一天，大象由主人牵着路过裁缝店时，它看见裁缝蜷缩在一张低矮的桌子上。他鼾声大作，根本没有看见大象。裁缝店旁边有一条路边的小溪。大象吸进鼻子里一些水，又把水全都喷到了正在睡觉的敌人的脸上。

裁缝被惊醒了，发现自己的衣服和店全都湿了。他正要捡起一根棍子打大象时，来了一群人。从人群中走出一个小男孩，对大象的主人说："先生，我曾亲眼看见这个裁缝对大象是多么凶残！"

❶ senseless
/ˈsenslɪs/
adj. 愚蠢的
❷ tease
/tiːs/
v. 捉弄
❸ prod
/prod/
v. 捅
❹ tempting
/ˈtemptɪŋ/
adj. 诱人的

The crowd then shouted that the tailor deserved[5] what the elephant had done to him.

The tailor was ashamed and he apologized and said he would no longer play any tricks on the elephant.

Moral：Don't do to others what you would not want them to do to you. Even animals can be hurt.

人们叫嚷着说大象这样对裁缝是他罪有应得。

裁缝很惭愧，道歉说他不会再捉弄大象了。

寓意：己所不欲，勿施于人。动物也有可能受伤害。

❺ **deserved**

/dɪˈzɜːvd/

adj. 该受的，应得的

The dog hero

英雄狗

It was as if Keeper was begging him not to drive him away from the house.

"守护者"好像在乞求他不要把自己从这个家赶出去。

Keeper was a lovely shaggy[1] dog that lived at a big farmhouse where there were two boys and a little girl to admire and pet him. Although Keeper loved the children, the one he loved best of all was Mary, the youngest of the family. And how little Mary loved Keeper. Wherever Mary went Keeper would follow. That was why he was called Keeper as he was always keeping his eyes on Mary.

In the mornings, Keeper would take Mary to school and go for her when it was time for her to leave and bring her home safely. However, when Mary was not around, the two brothers who attended the afternoon school stayed home with Keeper. They were rather mischievous[2] and liked to tease Keeper. "Keeper," the boys would say, "we will train you and if you see anyone annoying Mary or anyone of us, we will blow this whistle twice 'peep' 'peep.' Then you must bark fiercely and give chase after the person."

Keeper was gentle with the children and he did not mind letting them play with him as much as they liked. Little Mary loved to dress him up in her doll's bonnet. He was just a part of the family.

But Keeper could be fierce. He hated anyone who wore a uniform of any kind. Be it a policeman, a postman, a nurse or the butcher boy in his blue tunic[3] and apron. And more than once, the children's father had to pay for some damages that Keeper caused. In fact the neighbors began to hate that horrid dog, Keeper.

"守护者"是一只粗毛狗，住在一个大农场里，那里有两个男孩和一个小女孩夸它、宠它。虽然"守护者"很爱孩子们，但它最爱的还是玛丽，家里最小的一个。小玛丽也非常爱"守护者"呢！玛丽去哪里，"守护者"就跟到哪里。正因为它总是守护着玛丽，所以，它被称为"守护者"。

每天早上，"守护者"都送玛丽去上学，等她要放学时就去找她，把她安全带回家。然而，玛丽不在家的时候，上下午课的两兄弟就与"守护者"一起待在家里。他们特别顽皮，喜欢捉弄"守护者"。"'守护者'"，孩子们会说，"我们要训练训练你，如果你看见有人骚扰玛丽或我们两个，我吹两声口哨，你就凶狠地叫着去追他。"

"守护者"对孩子很温柔，只要他们喜欢，它并不介意跟他们玩。小玛丽就喜欢把她的布娃娃的帽子给它戴上。它就是这个家庭的一部分。

但是，"守护者"也有凶狠的时候。它讨厌所有穿制服的人，不管是警察、邮递员，还是穿着紧身短上衣、系着围裙的肉店伙计。曾经不止一次，孩子们的爸爸不得不为"守护者"造成的伤害做出赔偿。事实上，邻居们开始讨厌那只可怕的狗，"守护

❶ shaggy
/ˈʃægɪ/
adj. 粗毛的

❷ mischievous
/ˈmɪstʃɪvəs/
adj. 顽皮的，淘气的

❸ tunic
/ˈtjuːnɪk/
n. 紧身短上衣

One day as the boys were coming down the road, they saw a fat man who came out of his car to retrieve his hat which accidentally fell out while he was driving. He was about to grab the hat in his hand when the strong breeze blew the hat right in front of the boys' feet. When they saw the fat man who could hardly walk boys laughed. Instead of giving the hat to its owner, the boys took out the whistle and Keeper heard "peep" "peep." He immediately dashed off chasing after the man. The fat man could not run that he fell and was hurt. The boys again laughed and blew their whistle and shouted, "Keeper, let's go home." The boys ran as fast as they could with Keeper chasing after them.

How angry the fat man was and the matter was reported to the police. The next day the boys' laughter turned to sorrow when their father was told that his dog, Keeper, was dangerous and that he must get rid of it.

"Get rid of Keeper," the children cried and they pleaded with their father but to no avail. Poor little Mary was inconsolable[4] and she cried for many days. The two boys were sorry for what they had done to the fat man but it was too late. Their father was firm, "Keeper has to go," he told them sternly. In the evening after the children were in bed, a police van came and took Keeper away to journey some eighteen kilometers away to a place the children would never find or see him again. They missed Keeper very much and life was never the same without Keeper.

者".

　　有一天，男孩们在路上走着，看见一个
胖男人下车去捡他开车时掉出来的帽子。正
当他要伸手去抓帽子时，一股强风正好把帽
子吹到了男孩们的脚下。看到这个胖男人几
乎无法走路时，他们笑了起来。男孩们并没
有把帽子还给它的主人，而是拿出了口哨。
"守护者"听到两声口哨声，立即冲上去追
那个人。胖男人跑不动，跌倒了，还受了
伤。男孩们又笑了起来，吹着口哨喊道：
"'守护者'，我们回家吧。"男孩们使劲地快
跑，"守护者"跟在后面。

　　胖男人非常生气，把这件事告到了警察
局。第二天，警察对男孩们的爸爸说他的
狗，"守护者"，很危险，必须把它弄走。
这里，他们的笑声变成了痛苦。

　　"把'守护者'弄走。"孩子们哭着说。
他们请求爸爸的谅解，但根本没用。可怜的
小玛丽一连哭了好多天怎么安慰也不行。两
个男孩很后悔对那个胖男人所做的事，但已
经太晚了。他们的爸爸很坚决，"'守护者'
必须离开。"他严厉地对他们说。晚上，等
孩子们都睡了之后，来了一辆警车，把"守
护者"带到了一个 18 公里外的地方，孩子
们再也不会找到、也不会见到它了。他们都

❹ inconsolable
/ˌɪnkənˈsəuləbl/
adj. 无法安慰的

One morning while Mary was ready for breakfast, she opened the front door to collect the morning papers when she saw her beloved Keeper. "What are you doing and how did you come here," Mary asked as she hugged and kissed Keeper over and over again. Keeper's feet was swollen and bleeding badly. When the boys saw Keeper they too hugged him. But Keeper's sad eyes were focused at the master of the house, the children' father. It was as if Keeper was begging him not to drive him away from the house. The children's mother quickly came to the rescue and said, "Keeper shall stay with us, we will never send him away."

Shortly after, a policeman came knocking at the door. The family was surprised to hear that Keeper saved him when he was confronted by a dangerous escaped convict[5] who had tried to enter the van while it stopped at a petrol station. The policeman noticed that the van door was slightly opened. He went to inspect it when he saw the convict. He had no time to draw out his gun and luckily found a whistle in his pocket. He quickly blew it to draw attention as there were several cars parked nearby. The convict who had a knife wanted to hurl[6] it at him. Keeper who heard the whistle blew "peep" "peep" caught hold of one of the convict's legs and held it tightly. The policeman, with the aid of people who also heard the whistle blew, confronted the convict and he was handcuffed. Meantime as the van door was opened, Keeper ran away and was nowhere to be found.

"You are our hero, Keeper," the policeman said as he stroked

非常想念"守护者"，没有了"守护者"的日子和以前大不一样了。

　　一天早上，玛丽正准备吃早饭。她打开前门去拿早上的报纸，却发现了她心爱的"守护者"。"你在这里干什么？你是怎么回来的？"玛丽抱着它一遍遍地吻着。"守护者"的脚都肿了，流血流得很厉害。男孩们见到"守护者"时也都拥抱了它。但是，"守护者"悲伤的眼神却落在了一家之主、孩子们的爸爸的身上。"守护者"好像在乞求他不要把自己从这个家赶出去。孩子们的妈妈马上出来解围说："'守护者'要和我们在一起，我们再也不会把它赶走了。"

　　没过多久，一位警察来敲门。听到警察说"守护者"救了他一命，全家人都很惊讶。当时，一个在逃犯想进入停在加油站的警车，这个警察注意到车门被轻轻打开了。他去察看时，突然看见了罪犯。他没有时间去拔枪，却幸运地在口袋里找到了一支口哨。他迅速吹了口哨以引起注意，因为附近停了好几辆车。持刀的罪犯想把刀朝他扔过来。"守护者"听到口哨声后咬住了罪犯的腿，并紧紧咬住不放。在同样听到口哨声的人们的帮助下，警察与罪犯对抗，并把他铐了起来。这个时候，车门是开着的，"守护

❺ convict
/ˈkɒnvɪkt/
n. 罪犯

❻ hurl
/hɜːl/
v. 猛投

Keeper gently, "You saved my life. My chief inspector sent me to look for you. You have walked a long way home. When your legs are fully recovered, we will send a van to take you and your family to our station. There will be a party in your honor."

Keeper was no longer fierce with the man and women in uniform. In fact, he loved them all. He was later given a policeman's uniform, which was tailored to fit his size with the words "Hero" inscribed[7] on its pocket and a hat to match it. All the neighbors no longer hated Keeper and they came to see his uniform and hat, which the family proudly displayed in a beautiful glass case.

On special occasions, Keeper would be dressed in his policeman's uniform and both children and adults loved to be photographed with Keeper, the dog-hero.

Moral: Be kind to animals and a dog is indeed a man's best friend.

者"就跑了，到处都找不到它。

"你是我们的英雄，'守护者'，"警察边说边轻轻地抚摸着"守护者"，"你救了我的命，检察长派我来找你。你走了这么远的路才回到家，等你的腿全愈之后，我们会派车来，把你和你的家人接到我们局里来，我们要为你举办一次晚会。"

"守护者"对穿制服的男人、女人都不再凶狠了。事实上，它很爱他们。后来，他们为它量身定做了一套警服，口袋上写着"英雄"的字样，还配有一顶帽子。邻居们也都不再讨厌"守护者"，都来看它那被全家人骄傲地摆在玻璃柜里的制服和帽子。

在一些特殊的场合，"守护者"就会穿上它的警服，孩子和大人都喜欢与英雄狗"守护者"合影。

寓意：善待动物，狗的确是人类最好的朋友。

❼ inscribe

/ɪnˈskraɪb/

v. 题写

Three brothers and the beggar

三个兄弟和一个乞丐

Your parents' benevolence will be rewarded.

你父母的善行会得到回报的。

There were three poor brothers who inherited a pear tree. Each owned an equal share of the fruits that grew on it. They each took turns to tend the tree.

One day, a beggar came and going to the brothers, at different times, he asked for some fruits.

"Take these pears," said each brother in turn, "they are my share of the fruit but I cannot give you what belongs to my brothers." The beggar was pleased with the brothers' kindness and generosity. The beggar, though poorly dressed possessed mysterious power. He asked each brother separately what he would like as a gift.

The first brother said, "I would like a flourishing[1] vineyard." The beggar led him through a mountain pass and showed him the most flourishing vineyard of apples, pears and grapes. A dozen strong workmen were tending the vineyard.

The same question was asked of the second brother. "I want a fine flock of sheep and goats," he said. To another path the beggar showed him a fine flock of sheep browsing[2] and the goats being milked by women. These are all for you."

It came to the third brother's turn to answer, "I want only a true, pure and good maiden for a wife." The beggar was surprised, as he could not produce such a woman immediately. "If you don't mind," the beggar said, "I will be on the look out for the maiden as you

贫穷的三兄弟继承了一棵梨树，树上结的果实，每个人都有等量的一份。他们轮流照看着这棵树。

一天，来了一个乞丐。他分别向三兄弟要点儿水果。

"吃梨吧，"每个人都说，"这是我那一份，但我不能把属于我兄弟们的给你。"对于三兄弟的友善和慷慨，乞丐感到很高兴。乞丐尽管衣衫褴褛，却有种神奇的力量。他分别问三兄弟想要什么礼物。

老大说："我想要一个茂盛的果园。"乞丐带他翻过一座山，指给他看结满苹果、梨和葡萄的茂盛的果园，12名身强力壮的工人在照料着果园。

老二也被问了同样的问题。"我想要一大群山羊、绵羊。"他说。乞丐朝另一条路指给他看一大群正在吃草的绵羊和山羊，妇女们正在给羊挤奶。"这些都是你的了。"

轮到老三回答了，"我想要一个真实、纯洁的好姑娘作妻子。"乞丐很惊讶，因为他不能马上找到这样一个女子。"如果你不介意，"乞丐说，"我会留意帮你寻找你描述的那样的姑娘。""谢谢你，这段时间里，我会很耐心的。"老三回答。

① flourishing
/ˈflʌrɪʃɪŋ/
adj. 茂盛的
② browse
/braʊz/
v. 吃草

described. "Thank you and I will, meantime, be patient," replied the third brother.

But not long after, the beggar brought a beautiful and good woman. The young man liked what he saw. The maiden and the third brother were wedded. She was content to live in his old house. The couple worked hard and they took good care of their one and only pear tree.

After a year had passed, the beggar, disguised[3] in poorer rags, looking tired and weary, appeared before the brothers. They did not recognize him at all. He went to the first brother whose vineyard had flourished with all kinds of fruits. "Can I have a few of your grapes?" the beggar asked. The haughty man shooed[4] the beggar away and shouted, "If I gave grapes to every beggar, I would have nothing left." "Come with me," said the beggar as he dragged the man along, "You are not worthy of the gifts and you must go back to your poverty. Because of your selfishness, everything is lost to you."

The beggar then went to the brother who had received the flocks. "Can you give me a little of the goat's milk?" This brother screamed, "My milk has been contracted[5] to a farmer. The little milk that is left is for my family!" As a matter of fact, his flocks had multiplied tenfold. The beggar pulled the brother away and brought him to where the flocks of sheep and goats were. "Run away! " shouted the beggar and the flocks scattered and ran off and the man never saw them again.

但是，没过多久，乞丐就领来了一位漂亮的好姑娘，年轻人看了之后很喜欢。姑娘和老三结了婚，住在他的老房子里，她感到很满足。这对夫妇辛勤耕作，细心照料着他们仅有的那棵梨树。

一年过去了，乞丐穿着更加破旧的衣服出现在疲惫不堪地三兄弟面前，他们根本没有认出他来。老大的果园里已经长满了各种各样的水果，乞丐来到了他跟前。"我能吃几粒葡萄吗?"乞丐问。这个高傲的人发着嘘嘘声把乞丐赶走了，并喊道："如果每个乞丐我都给他葡萄吃，我就什么都不剩了。""跟我来，"乞丐边说边拽着这个人走，"你不配得到这些礼物，你必须回到你的贫困中去。由于你的自私，你会失去一切。"

接着，乞丐来到得到了羊群的老二的面前。"你能给我一点儿羊奶喝吗?"老二尖叫着说："我的羊奶承包给了一个农民，剩下的一点儿是留给我们全家人喝的!"事实上，他的羊群已经扩大了10倍。乞丐拉着老二到羊群所在的地方。"去吧!"乞丐大声喊。羊群散开了，羊全跑了，这个人再也没有见到过它们。

❸ **disguise**
/dɪsˈɡaɪz/
v. 伪装
❹ **shoo**
/ʃuː/
v. 发着嘘赶
❺ **contract**
/kənˈtrækt/
v. 承包

The beggar went to the third brother. The man caught sight of the beggar, and said, "You're welcome to share our food with us. My wife will be happy to bake you a cake. We also have a pear for you! " Turning to the lady, the beggar enquired, "I see you are pregnant[6]! When is the baby due?" "The baby is due any-time," she replied.

After the beggar had his fill, he thanked the couple and re-marked that the pear tree is bare. "Each time the tree bear fruits, we give them to our poor neighbors as they are in more need than us. We always keep a pear or two in case some stranger come along unexpectedly."

That night the beggar slept soundly on the bed of fresh straw the couple laid for him. But he was awoken when the husband rushed excitedly and told him that his wife was having labor pains. "Can you help me to call our neighbor to come quickly? I will boil a kettle of water so it will be ready when she comes. She knows what to do! "

The husband and the beggar waited until they heard the baby's cry. "You have a healthy baby boy," the neighbor announced happily. The beggar stayed until all the commotion[7] was over.

This time before he left, he congratulated the couple. And in a dignified sage like manner, he took the baby in his arms and said, "Your parents' benevolence will be rewarded. You will bring them luck as well as your brothers and sisters who will come after

乞丐来到老三面前。他看见了乞丐，说："欢迎你与我们一起用餐。我妻子会很高兴为你烤一块蛋糕的。我们还给你留了一个梨！"乞丐转向那女士说："我看你好像怀孕啦！什么时候生啊？""就快生了。"她回答。

乞丐吃饱后，答谢了这对夫妇，又说梨树上光秃秃的。"每年树上结了果实，我们就把果实送给邻居们，因为他们比我们更加困苦。我们总是留下一两个梨，以防万一有什么想不到的陌生人会来。"

那天晚上，乞丐躺在夫妇俩为他铺好的干草席上睡得特别香。但是后来他被吵醒了，因为丈夫兴冲冲地跑进来告诉他说妻子要临产了。"你能帮我去叫邻居马上过来吗？我要烧一壶开水，等她来的时候就要把水准备好。她知道该怎么做！"

丈夫和乞丐一直等到听到了婴儿的啼哭声。"你得了个大胖小子。"邻居高兴地宣布。等到这件事完全平息之后，乞丐才离开。

在离开之前，他向这对夫妇道了贺。他把孩子抱在怀里，举止如高尚的圣人一般，说道："你父母的善行会得到回报的。你和你所有的弟弟妹妹们都将给他们带来好运。"乞丐把孩子还给母亲时又补充说："我留下了一

⑥ pregnant
/ˈpregnənt/
adj. 怀孕的

⑦ commotion
/kəˈməʊʃən/
n. 混乱，骚动

you." As the beggar returned the baby to his mother, he added, "I have left a little gift. Do not open the bag until I am gone." The couple was so busy with the baby, they forgot about the gift.

One day as the wife was cleaning up the room, she noticed the bag. "Husband, come quickly and see what's in it!" They were shocked to find that it was full of golden coins. The beggar's prediction came true!

The pear tree bore luscious[8] fruits all year round. The couple's four children took turns to tend the tree. Like their parents, they also shared its fruits with their school friends, neighbors and anyone who happened to be passing by.

个小礼物，等我走之后再打开它。"夫妇俩忙着照顾孩子，竟把礼物的事忘了。

有一天，妻子在打扫房间时发现了这个袋子。"老公，快来看里面有什么！"他们吃惊地发现里面竟装满了金币。乞丐的话变成现实啦！

梨树上全年都结满了甜美的果实。这对夫妇的4个孩子轮流照看着梨树。他们也像父母一样，与同学邻居及任何碰巧路过的人们分享着自己的果实。

❽ luscious

/ˈlʌʃəs/

adj. 甘美的

Mr. Pitch

沥青先生

I may be black outside but my heart inside is white.

可能我的外表是黑的，但我的内心却是白的。

What Mr. Pitch was really called, Tony did not know. Everybody called him Mr. Pitch. It was rumored[1] that his face and hands were black as ink, and his teeth and eyes looked very white. Mr. Pitch always carried a long black brush on his shoulder. In fact, neither Tony nor any of the children had ever met Mr. Pitch.

All the children were interested in him. So the image of Mr. Pitch carried on. Some of them were a little afraid of him. But Tony's little sister, Dottie was most afraid of Mr. Pitch. That was because Tony who was two years older, often said to her: "You better hurry up, slow coach or you will certainly have Mr. Pitch after you." "What would he do if he got me?" Dottie would ask. "Take you to the chimney where he lives and feed you on soot[2] soup," replied Tony.

Tony kept telling her stories of the horrors that went on in Mr. Pitch's chimney. "I heard that he prowled[3] around at night with a great big bag, and would catch the children and put them in the bag." Although Tony had scared her out of her wits and Dottie was shivering, she managed to ask, "Why didn't the policeman catch Mr. Pitch and put him in jail? Papa says anyone who is mean would be put there." "Don't worry, your brave brother will always protect you," Tony said proudly. He would then flexed up[4] his muscles to show how strong he was which made Dottie laugh.

When Dottie's sixth birthday came, her mother said she was old enough to go to school and Tony volunteered to take her. Indeed, Tony took great care of her and he always waited for her after

沥青先生的真名是什么，托尼并不知道。大家都叫他沥青先生。有传言说他的脸和手黑如墨，而牙齿和眼睛却很白。沥青先生肩上总是扛着一个长长的黑刷子。事实上，不管是托尼还是别的孩子，谁也没碰到过沥青先生。

所有的孩子都对沥青先生很感兴趣。他的形象就这样继续流传下去。有些孩子有点儿害怕沥青先生，但是，托尼的小妹妹多蒂却非常怕他。正因为如此，比她大两岁的托尼常对多蒂说："你最好快点儿，磨蹭虫，否则，沥青先生会来追你的。""如果他抓住我，会把我怎么样呢？"多蒂会问。"把你带到他住的烟囱里，给你喝煤烟粥。"托尼回答。

托尼总是给她讲一些发生在沥青先生的烟囱里的恐怖故事。"我听说夜里他背着个大袋子四处游荡抓小孩子，然后把他们装到袋子里。"尽管托尼把多蒂吓得魂不附体，浑身发抖，她还是会说："为什么警察不逮捕沥青先生，把他关进监狱呢？爸爸说，坏蛋都会被关到那儿去。""别担心，你勇敢的哥哥会一直保护你的。"托尼自豪地说。接着，他收缩起肌肉，来显示他有多么强壮，这把多蒂逗笑了。

❶ rumor
/ˈruːmə/
v. 传言
❷ soot
/suːt/
n. 煤烟
❸ prowl
/praʊl/
v. 游荡
❹ flex up
收缩

school and brought her home safely. But Dottie still lived in one long terror. Whenever they came to a cross road, Tony would say: "I wonder if we shall meet Mr. Pitch today?" At other times, he said that they should run home, "Dottie, did you hear his footsteps behind us?"

Time went by and Tony's horror stories about Mr. Pitch had shimmered down. Dottie was comforted that her brother would always protect her. But one day, Tony had a very bad headache and was sent home from school in the early afternoon. So when the bell rang and all the children went out with their bags, there was no one to take Dottie home. She forgot all about Mr. Pitch till she was at a cross road. As she looked around, her heart stood still. There he was, a tall big man, coming along close behind. Dottie started to run. Out of her schoolbag slipped her new reading book. Mr. Pitch saw it and picked it up.

"Hi, missie," he called out, "You've left your reading book." As Dotie took no notice, he decided to run after her. She gave a loud shriek and threw away her bag and fled. Mr. Pitch was surprised. He picked up the bag and continued running after her. At last Dottie's breath failed her. She had run on without knowing where she was going. The street was strange to her. She gave a cry, and at that moment, caught her foot on the curb[5] and rolled over on the hard stone road. Mr. Pitch was beside her. "By jolly, what have you done, missie? Why are you in such a hurry?" Dottie hid her face and sobbed, "Don't take me away, please Mr. Pitch! Don't! Please, please, Mr. Pitch!" "But your knee needs attending

到多蒂6岁时，妈妈说她长大了，该上学了，托尼自告奋勇去送她。托尼对她确实照顾得无微不至，放学后总是等她，把她安全带回家。但是，多蒂还是长期生活在恐惧之中。每到一个十字路口，托尼就会说："不知道今天我们会不会碰上沥青先生？"有时候，他还说他们应该跑着回家。"多蒂，你听到我们身后的脚步声了吗？"

时间一天天过去，托尼关于沥青先生的恐怖故事渐渐少了。有哥哥一直保护着，多蒂也感到很安慰。但是，有一天，托尼头疼得厉害，下午早早就被从学校送回了家。所以，下课铃响后，孩子们都背着书包出去了，没有人带多蒂回家。她根本没想起沥青先生这码事，但来到一个十字路口时，她回头看了看，心脏都停止了跳动。后面紧跟着一个人，高高大大的。多蒂开始跑了起来。她的新课本从书包里掉了出来，沥青先生看见了，把它拾了起来。

"喂，小姑娘，"他喊道，"你的课本掉了。"由于多蒂没有理会他，他决定去追她。她尖叫了一声，扔下书包，撒腿就跑。沥青先生感到很惊讶。他捡起书包，继续追她。最后，多蒂喘不过气来了。她一直在跑，却不知道在往哪儿跑。她不认识这条街。她哭

❺ curb

/kɜːb/

n. (街道的)镶边石

to," he said, "I'll tend to your wound and then take you home."

He took her up gently in his arms. Dottie gave one sob after another. She closed her eyes as Mr. Pitch was carrying her away to his chimney. She heard him open a door and then she was set down carefully on something soft. She heard taps of running water. It took her a while before she dared to open her eyes. She found herself in a nice little room. A fire burned brightly and a yellow canary[6] sang sweet songs in a cage. Then Mr. Pitch came; drying his hands and gave her a big smile.

Dottie gave a big sigh. "Are you Mr. Pitch? Why, you've such a beautiful dark skin and your teeth are so white! You're not white like Mr. Glum, my music teacher! " "What do you mean, missie? Do you think all black men are wicked[7]? I may be black outside but my heart inside is white."

Dottie and Mr. Pitch soon started to talk and Dottie narrated what Tony, her brother, told her. "I never knew that the imaginary figure your brother and the children invented was directed at me. But I like the name Mr. Pitch and I'll stick to it." Dottie and her new found friend, Mr. Pitch, had a jolly good laugh. After a hot cup of tea and some chocolates, Mr. Pitch took her home. She even kissed him lightly on his cheeks and said, "Mr. Pitch you're the nicest person I've met. I'll never forget you." Dottie did not say anything to Tony about Mr. Pitch. But that night she told her mother all that had happened and how Mr. Pitch nursed her wounded knee.

了起来，就在那一刹那，她的一只脚却被路沿绊住，摔倒在了坚硬的石板路上。沥青先生就在她身旁。"天哪，你干了什么，小姑娘？为什么这么着急？""千万别把我带走，求你了，沥青先生！别！求求你，求求你，沥青先生！""可是你的膝盖需要包扎一下，"他说，"我给你包一下伤口，然后带你回家。"

他轻轻地把她抱在怀里。多蒂一声接一声地啜泣着。当沥青先生带她到他的烟囱里去时，她闭上了双眼。她听见他打开了一扇门，然后自己被小心地放在了什么软东西上。她听见了水龙头的声音。过了一会，她才敢睁开眼睛，发现自己在一间漂亮的小屋里，炉火烧得正旺，笼子里的金丝雀唱着动听的歌。这时候，沥青先生来了；他擦干手，冲她灿烂地一笑。

多蒂深深地叹了口气。"你是沥青先生吗？怎么，你的黑皮肤好漂亮，牙齿好白啊！你不是像我的音乐老师格兰姆先生一样的白人！""你这是什么意思，小姑娘？你认为所有黑人都是坏人吗？可能我的外表是黑的，但我的内心却是白的。"

很快，多蒂和沥青先生就攀谈了起来，多蒂讲了哥哥托尼给她讲的故事。"我从不知道你哥哥和那些孩子们编出来的虚构的人

❻ canary

/kəˈneərɪ/

n. 金丝雀

❼ wicked

/ˈwɪkɪd/

adj. 罪恶的

The next day when they were reaching home from school, Tony said, "Hurry up you slow coach or Mr Pitch will be after you," Dottie did not utter a word. But when they reached the cross road, there right before them stood Mr. Pitch carrying a canary. It was Tony's turn to run and when she caught up with her brother calmly said, "Mr. Pitch will be coming to tea. Mama has invited him."

Moral: What if a man is white, black, red, yellow or tan! The outside may be different but we <u>belong to</u>[8] the family of man.

物指的就是我。但是，我喜欢沥青先生这个
名字，以后就用它了。"多蒂和她的新朋友
沥青先生开怀大笑起来。喝了一杯热茶，又
吃了一些巧克力之后，沥青先生带她回了
家。她甚至还轻轻地吻了他的脸颊，说：
"沥青先生，你是我遇到的最好的人，我不
会忘记你的。"有关沥青先生的事，多蒂对
托尼只字未提。但是，那天晚上，她把发生
的一切，以及沥青先生怎么护理她受伤的膝
盖告诉了妈妈。

第二天，他们放学回家时，托尼说：
"快点儿，磨蹭虫，否则沥青先生会来追你
的。"多蒂一句话也没有说。但是，当他们
到了十字路口时，沥青先生就站在他们面
前，手里托着金丝雀。这次轮到托尼逃跑
了。她赶上哥哥后，镇静地说："沥青先生
要来喝茶，妈妈已经邀请他了。"

寓意：人的皮肤是白色、黑色、红色、
黄色或褐色又如何？我们的外表可能不同，
但我们都属于人类这个大家庭。

❽ belong to
属于

A man of peace

和平之人

It must be for the animals that God allows the sun to shine and the rain to fall in a country whose men are so base and unworthy of such great blessings.

一定是因为这些动物，上帝才把阳光雨露洒在这个国家的，因为那里的人们那么卑鄙，不配得到这么多的神恩。

When Alexander the Great was engaged in his conquering march through the East, he came to a tribe living in a secluded[1] spot far from the eyes of men. These people lived a very simple life. They knew neither war nor conquest; all their arts were of peace.

Alexander was once led to the hut of the chief, who received him with great hospitality and ordered a plate of fruit to be set before him. The chief heard that Alexander should only be served with some fine food not found in his country. When the dish was brought, great was Alexander's astonishment. It was not something fit to eat but a number of dates all made of gold.

"Golden dates! " said Alexander. "Do you eat gold in this country?" "Oh, no! But as fruits must certainly grow in your country as it does here, I thought that you would be happy with the dish of golden dates! If you can't eat them perhaps you would want to take them back with you! " the chief replied.

"I'm not interested in your gold, I have enough of this at home." Alexander replied angrily. "But have you ever eaten golden dates?" the chief asked. "Certainly not! " Alexander then knew what the chief implied and he changed the subject.

"You are so far away from civilization, I'm only interested to know something of your manners and customs." "You're welcome to stay with me and you shall learn all you wish to know." A short time afterwards, two tribesmen came into the chief's hut to settle their dispute.

亚历山大大帝东征之时，来到了一个人迹罕至的部落。那里的人们过着简朴的生活。他们不知道打仗和战争；所有的技艺都是用于和平的。

有一次，亚历山大被带到了部落首领的小屋里。族长热情地接待了他，并下令为他上一盘水果。族长听说只能用亚历山大的国家没有的某种精美食品来招待他。盘子端上来的时候，亚历山大吃了一惊。这根本不是什么能吃的东西，而是许多金子做成的枣。

"金枣！"亚历山大说，"你们国家的人吃金子吗？""噢不！但是，既然这里的水果肯定你的国家也有，我原以为来一盘金枣你可能会很高兴！如果不能吃，大概你想把它们带回去吧！"族长回答。

"我对你的金子没有兴趣，我家里多得是，"亚历山大气愤地回答。"但是，你吃过金枣吗？"族长问。"当然没有！"后来，亚历山大知道了族长的意思，就转换了话题。

"你们与文明社会相隔甚远，我只想了解一下你们的礼貌和习俗。""欢迎你和我待在一起，你会如愿以偿的。"不一会儿，两个族人到族长的小屋来解决争端。

"族长，我从这个人手中买了一块地。在挖排水沟时，我发现了埋在地下的财宝。

1 secluded
/sɪˈkluːdɪd/
adj. 人迹罕至的

"Chief, I bought a piece of land from this man. As I was digging a ditch[2] to drain it, I found a treasure of gold that lay buried beneath the seller's surface. I wanted to return the treasure to him but he refused to accept it. My conscience does not allow me to keep what is not mine."

"The other tribesman said, "Chief, I sold him the land with all its future and present benefits so naturally the treasure belongs to him now."

Each tribesman was adamant[3] that he was right. Finally, after much argument both man came to this conclusion and said, "Chief, we know you're a man of peace. You will treat our case justly so we will accept your verdict[4] without further contradiction."

"Alright, I believe you have an only son?" "Yes," replied the tribesman. "And you I know have a beautiful daughter." "Yes, I have a daughter." "Then let your son marry his daughter and bestow the treasure upon them as a marriage gift," said the chief. To one tribesman, he said, "In order to have peace in the home, please go and consult your son and his mother, your wife." To the other, "You go and consult your daughter and your wife too," as he dismissed the two tribesmen.

Alexander was so impressed with what he had witnessed. "Do you think my decision is unjust?" "Oh no! I am greatly surprised because I have never heard of anything like this before. It took you only a few moments to settle the matter."

我想把财宝还给他，但他不要。我的良心不允许我拿不属于自己的东西。"

另一个族人说："族长，我把土地连同它现在、将来的收益一起卖给了他，所以，财宝现在自然属于他。"

两个人都坚持说自己是对的，最后，两个人经过一番争吵之后得出结论说："族长，我们知道您是和平之人。您会公正处理我们这件事的，所以，我们愿意接受您的裁决，不再反对。"

"那好吧。你有一个独生子，是不是？""是的。"一个族人回答。"我知道你有一个漂亮的女儿。""对，我是有一个女儿。"另一名族人回答。"那么让你的儿子娶他的女儿，把财宝作为结婚礼物送给他们。"族长说。他对一个族人说："要想家庭和睦，请去问你的儿子和他的妈妈，就是你的妻子。"他又对另一个族人说："你也去问你的女儿和妻子。"说着，他便打发两个族人走了。

亚历山大所目睹的一切给他留下了深刻印象。"你觉得我的决定不公正吗？""噢，不！我很吃惊，因为我以前从没听说过这样的事。解决这件事你才花了几分钟的时间。"

"在你的国家里，你那些高明的人们会如何处理这样的事呢？"族长问。"坦白地

② **ditch**
/dɪtʃ/
n. 水沟

③ **adamant**
/ˈædəmənt/
adj. 坚决的

④ **verdict**
/ˈvɜːdɪkt/
n. 裁决

"How would your wise men decide in such a case in your country?" enquired the chief. "To tell you honestly, we would have both parties arrested and seized the treasure for the king's use," replied Alexander.

It was the chief's turn to reply in astonishment. "Does the sun of the heavens shine on your country?" "Certainly! " "How wonderful," replied the chief. "And does the gentle rain fall there too?" "Of course." Again, the chief remarked, "How wonderful! "

Then the chief sat in deep thought while Alexander wondered why he had asked the questions about the sun and the rain. At last the chief spoke, "But are there tame animals that live on grass?" he asked. "Many of them." "Ah," said the chief, "then it must be for the animals that God allows the sun to shine and the rain to fall in a country whose men are so base[5] and unworthy of such great blessings."

Alexander the Great was also known as the Conqueror[6]. It was said when he was dying, he asked that his right hand be placed upright out from the coffin before burial . Why? An indication that in spite of the treasures and lands he conquered, he had to leave everything behind and could not take them with him.

Which of the two would you like as your role model? Alexander the Great or the chief, a man of peace?

说，我们会逮捕双方，然后把财宝抢来献给国王，"亚历山大回答。

这一次轮到族长感到诧异了。"天上的太阳照耀着你的国家吗?""当然!""多好啊，"族长说。"那里也会降下温和的细雨吗?""当然!""多好啊!"族长又说。

后来，族长坐在那里沉思，而亚历山大却不知道族长为什么会问他太阳和雨的问题。最后，族长开口了："可是，那里有驯服的食草动物吗?"他问。"很多。""啊，"族长说，"那么，一定是因为这些动物，上帝才把阳光雨露洒在这个国家的，因为那里的人们那么卑鄙，不配得到这么多的神恩。"

亚历山大大帝又被称为征服者。据说，在临死之前，他要求在葬礼前把他的右手伸到棺材外面。为什么呢? 这意味着尽管他攻城掠地，掠夺财宝无数，却只能留在身后，什么也带不走。

二者之中，你愿以谁为榜样呢? 是亚历山大大帝、还是族长这位和平之人?

❺ base
/beɪs/
adj. 卑鄙的
❻ conqueror
/ˈkɒŋkərə/
n. 征服者

Do clothes make a man?
人靠衣装吗？

*O mighty garments, you are esteemed above all
else in this world...*

噢，伟大的衣服啊，你比世界上其他所有
东西都尊贵……

A Brahmin, a member of the Hindu priest, had a great reputation for holiness, and received many presents so that he became rich. One day, he took a fancy to dress himself as a poor peasant. In this attire[1], he went into the market place but no one saluted him and no one gave him any presents.

The Brahmin then returned to his house and, dressing himself in rich garments, once more set out for the market place. This time, everybody saluted him and made way for him and many handed him presents. This was the usual custom when a holy Brahmin happened to make his appearance in the market place.

Once again, the Brahmin returned to his home and changed his clothes. Then, taking the rich garments, he set them up on a shrine near the market. As he prostrates[2] himself before them, cried continually: "O mighty garments, you are esteemed above all else in this world..."

The people gathered round in wonder, and in time came to worship the clothes as this Brahmin was doing. This custom has spread farther and farther. Now in many countries around the world, trendy[3] and fashionable people do the same thing, though not, perhaps in the way as the Brahmin did.

Moral: Look at the lilies in the muddy pond! How beautifully dressed they grow!

一位婆罗门，印度僧侣之一，在圣洁方面享有极高的威望，所以他收到了很多礼物，也因此变得很富有。一天，他突然把自己打扮成了一个贫穷的农民。他穿着这身衣服去了集市上，但是，没有人向他行礼，也没有人送给他礼物。

婆罗门回到家里，穿上华丽的衣服，又去了集市上。这一次，每个人都向他行礼，给他让路，还有许多人送他礼物。按照习俗，神圣的婆罗门出现在集市上时人们通常都会这样做。

婆罗门又回家换了身衣服，然后，他拿着这套华丽的衣服，把它架在了集市附近的一个圣坛上。他拜倒在衣服前面，口中念念有词："噢，伟大的衣服啊，你比世界上其他所有东西都尊贵……"

人们好奇地聚拢了过来，最后也都开始朝衣服膜拜，因为婆罗门在这样做。这一习俗已经传播得很远很远。现在，全世界许多国家赶时髦的人们都在做着这样的事，尽管可能与婆罗门的方式不同。

寓意：看看泥塘里的莲花吧！它们出落得多么美丽动人啊！

❶ attire
/əˈtaɪə/
n. 衣服
❷ prostrate
/prɒsˈtreɪt/
v. 跪拜
❸ trendy
/ˈtrendɪ/
adj. 时髦的

A clever donkey

聪明的驴

Life is going to shovel dirt on you, all kinds of dirt.

生活会往你身上铲土,各种各样的土。

One day a farmer's donkey fell down into a well. The animal cried piteously[1] for hours as the farmer tried to figure out what to do. Finally, he decided the animal was old, and the well needed to be covered up anyway; it just wasn't worth it to retrieve[2] the donkey.

He invited all his neighbors to come over and help him. They all grabbed a shovel and began to shovel dirt into the well. At first, the donkey realized what was happening and cried horribly. Then, to everyone's amazement he quieted down. A few shovel loads later, the farmer finally looked down the well. He was astonished at what he saw.

With each shovel of dirt that hit his back, the donkey was doing something amazing. He would shake it off and take a step up. As the farmer's neighbors continued to shovel dirt on top of the animal, he would shake it off and take a step up. Pretty soon, everyone was amazed as the donkey stepped up over the edge of the well and happily trotted off!

Life is going to shovel dirt on you, all kinds of dirt. The trick to getting out of the well is to shake it off and take a step up. Each of our troubles is a stepping-stone. We can get out of the deepest wells just by not stopping, never giving up! Shake it off and take a step up.

Remember the five simple rules to be happy:

有一天，农夫的驴掉进了井里。在农夫想办法的时候，可怜的驴叫了好几个小时。最后，农夫决定，驴已老了，反正井也需要填平；把驴救出来不太值得了。

他请了所有的邻居来帮忙。他们都抄起铲子，开始往井中铲土。开始，驴意识到发生了什么事，便发出了令人胆战心惊的叫声。后来，令大家奇怪的是，驴安静了下来。又填了几铲土之后，农夫往井里看了看。他见到的情景让他惊讶不已。

驴对砸在背上的每一铲土做出了非凡之举：他把土抖掉，然后往上走一步。随着农夫的邻居们不断往驴身上铲土，驴把土抖掉，再往上走一步。很快，每个人都惊呆了——驴迈出了井口，欢快地跑了！

生活会往你身上铲土，各种各样的土。从井里出来的办法就是抖掉土，往上走一步。我们的每一个困难都是一块垫脚石。通过不懈的努力，永不放弃，我们可以从最深的井里走出来！抖掉尘土，往上走一步。

谨记5条简单的快乐原则：

1. 解脱心灵，不要怨恨——宽恕

2. 放松大脑，不要焦虑——很多事情都不会发生

❶ piteously
/ˈpɪtɪəslɪ/
adv. 可怜地

❷ retrieve
/rɪˈtriːv/
v. 重新得到

1. Free your heart from hatred — Forgive.

2. Free your mind from worries — Most never happen.

3. Live simply and appreciate what you have.

4. Give more.

5. Expect less.

The donkey later came back and bit the shovel out of the farmer who had tried to bury him. The gash[3] from the bite got infected, and the farmer eventually died in agony from septic[4] shock.

Moral: When you do something wrong and try to cover your ass, it always come back to bite you.

3.简单生活，感谢所有

4.多给予

5.少要求

后来，驴出来了，把铲子从想埋葬他的农夫手中咬了出来。农夫被咬过的伤口感染了，最终，他在对感染的恐惧中痛苦地死去了。

寓意：如果你想掩盖做过的错事，终究会受到惩罚。

❸ gash

/gæʃ/

n. 砍得很深的伤口

❹ septic

/ˈseptɪk/

adj. 受感染的

The poor girl who became a queen
穷女孩变王后

If ever you want to get rid of me, that I be allowed to carry with me one thing I loved best.

如果你想抛弃我的话，请允许我带走一件我最喜欢的东西。

Once upon a time, in a small village lived a man who had a pretty daughter. Although she had never been to school, she was very wise. One day, the father went to see the King to ask a favor. As the father stood before the King, he did not shiver with fear or stammer[1]. His voice was clear and every word was well pronounced.

"Who taught you to speak so well?" "My daughter, your Majesty!" he replied. "Who taught your daughter to be so wise?" "She learned her wisdom from Heaven. I am too poor to send her to school."

"Well, let me put her to a test. Give her these eggs and if she does not lay chickens from them, I will put you both in prison."

The father returned and gave the eggs and told his daughter what the King said. "These are boiled eggs," the girl exclaimed. Then she took a pot and, filling it with water, put it on the fire and boiled a quantity of beans. "Father, take these beans go into the ploughed field. The King would usually pass that way and when you see him coming, spread and sow the beans and cry out, 'Heaven grant that these boiled beans may grow into fine, healthy crops.'"

When the King came along and heard the man's cry, he exclaimed: "You silly man, do you expect boiled beans to take root?" "As much as I expect boiled eggs to hatch into chickens." The King realized that his daughter advised the man. She had in

从前，在一个小村子里住着一个人，他漂亮的女儿虽然从没有上过学，却非常聪明。有一天，父亲去见国王请求恩典。父亲站在国王面前，既没有怕得发抖，说话也不结巴。他口齿清晰，每个字都讲得非常标准。

"是谁教你说得这么好的？" "是我女儿，陛下！"他回答。"是谁把你女儿教得这么聪明？" "她天生就很聪明。我家太穷了，没有钱送她上学。"

"好吧，让我来考考她。把这些鸡蛋交给她，如果她不能孵出小鸡来，我就把你们两个都关进监狱。"

父亲回来把鸡蛋交给了女儿，并把国王的话告诉了她。"这些鸡蛋是煮熟了的。"女孩说。于是，她拿来一只锅，盛满水后放在炉子上煮豆。"爸爸，把这些豆拿到犁过的地里去。每天早上国王通常都会经过那条路，你看到他来的时候，就把豆撒在地里，并大声说：'上帝说这些煮熟的豆能长成优质、茁壮的庄稼。'"

当国王过来听见这个人的喊声时，他说："你这个傻瓜，你指望煮熟的豆能生根吗？" "我还指望煮熟的鸡蛋能孵出小鸡来呢。"国

❶ stammer
/ˈstæmə/
v. 结巴

deed outwitted[2] him so he gave her another test.

"Take this wooden bowl and tell your daughter that with it, she must empty the ocean." This message was passed on to his daughter. She, in turn, handed her father a big bunch of wool. "Tell the King, with it he must stop up the sources of all the rivers and lakes. Then I would empty the ocean." The King was pleased to hear her wise answer. He decided to make her his Queen.

She told her father to take a note for the King. "Your Majesty, I am willing to marry you, but there's one condition you must agree. If ever you want to get rid of me, that I be allowed to carry with me one thing I loved best." The King consented and they were married.

After a year had passed, the King grew tired of her and wanted a new wife. "Tomorrow, O King, I will depart[3]. In accordance with your promise, I will take the one thing I love above all else. Come and spend our last night together. I would like to make a toast to your good health and happiness. The Queen mixed something secretly with the King's wine. He cheerfully drank the wine and wished her well too. The wine made the King drowsy and he soon fell asleep. The King slept soundly[4] all through the night. When he woke up in the morning, he rubbed his eyes in great astonishment.

"Where am I?" he shouted as he looked around him.

王意识到这个人受了他女儿的指点。她的确比自己聪明，所以国王又给她出了一道题。

"把这个木碗拿回去，告诉你女儿，她必须用这只木碗把大海淘干。"父亲把话告诉了女儿。她反过来给了父亲一大卷毛线，"告诉国王，他必须用这卷毛线拦截住所有江河湖泊的源泉。然后，我就会淘干海水。"国王听到她睿智的回答，感到很高兴。他决定娶她作王后。

她让父亲给国王带了张便条，"陛下，我很愿意嫁给你，但是，你必须答应我一个条件。如果你想抛弃我的话，请允许我带走一件我最喜欢的东西。"国王表示同意，他们就结婚了。

一年过去了，国王厌烦她了，想要娶一个新妻子。"噢，国王，明天我就要走了。按照你的承诺，我将带走一件我最喜欢的东西。来和我度过最后一个晚上吧，我要敬你一杯酒，祝你健康、幸福。"王后悄悄在国王的酒里搀了点儿东西。他高兴地喝了酒，也祝她一切都好。酒使国王昏昏欲睡，很快，他就睡着了。整个晚上他睡得都很香。早上醒来时，他惊讶地揉了揉眼睛。

❷ outwit
/aʊtˈwɪt/
v. 胜过，比⋯聪明

❸ depart
/dɪˈpɑːt/
v. 离开

❹ soundly
/ˈsaʊndlɪ/
adv. 非常好

"In my house," answered the Queen. "I have left the palace and in accordance with your command, I have taken with me what I love best."

"What treasure did you take?" the King asked. "My treasure is you, O my royal husband! "

The King was greatly touched. "I now understand how truly wise you are and what true love is. I don't want to lose you so please come back with me!" The King and his Queen returned to the palace and they lived happily ever after.

Moral: True love will surpassed[5] the test of time and is everlasting.

“我在哪儿?”他向四周看了看，说。

“在我家里，”王后回答，“我已经离开了王宫，按照你的命令，我带走了我的最爱。”

“你带了什么宝物?”国王问。“我的宝物就是你，我的国王丈夫!”

国王被深深地打动了。“现在，我明白了你是多么睿智，明白了什么才是真爱。我不想失去你，请和我一起回去吧!”国王和王后回到了王宫，从此过上了幸福生活。

寓意：真爱永恒，经得起时间的考验。

❺ **surpass**
/sɜːˈpaːs/
v. 超越，胜过

Control your tongue

管住你的舌头

You gossipers always blame someone else even after you have done the damage.

你们爱讲闲话的人总是责怪别人，即使损失是自己造成的。

One day, a rich lady went to a counselor[1] to ask his advice. She said she was in the habit of gossiping about people. She found it difficult to control her tongue. But what was more horrible was that her only daughter would often come home from school unhappy. "When I asked her why she was unhappy, she said, 'My friends said you, mother, is a busybody and a gossip! '"

"You can imagine how mad I was. I demanded to know the friend's name. Then I approached every parent who said such awful things about me to lay off my girl. But instead of making the situation better, it became worse. My girl now refuses to go to school as the whole class have boycotted[2] her."

"Sir, it is for my girl's sake as well as mine that I have sought your help."

"Before I can give any advice, I must find the root cause as to why you like to gossip," the counselor said.

The lady laughed hysterically[3]. "It began with my mother who was known as the town gossip. Mother says it keeps her entertained, as otherwise life would be dull. As a child, I too, would enjoy when mother meets up with the other gossipers and their stories went on and on. But it was done only while my father was not around as he traveled a lot for his work. Once father came home unexpectedly as someone complained to him about mother. 'Why don't you keep your mouth shut? Who would want to marry our child if she followed your footsteps?' he shouted. Mother never kept

有一天，一位贵夫人来找一位顾问寻求建议。她说她总是有说别人闲话的习惯，发现很难管住自己的舌头。但是，更可怕的是，她女儿放学回家时经常闷闷不乐。"我问她为什么会闷闷不乐，她说：'我的朋友们说，妈妈你是一个好管闲事、爱说闲话的人！'"

"你可以想像我有多生气。我要求知道这位朋友是谁。后来，我去找每一个这样说我坏话的家长，让他们不要再搔扰我的女儿。但是，情况非但没有好转，反而更加糟糕了。现在，我女儿拒绝去学校，因为全班同学都排斥她。"

"先生，为了我女儿，也为了我自己，我来寻求您的建议。"

"在给你建议之前，我必须找出你喜欢说闲话的根本原因。"顾问说。

这位夫人歇斯底里地笑了起来。"这源于我的妈妈，她是镇上有名的爱说闲话的人。妈妈说，说闲话令她很开心，否则，生活会枯燥乏味的。作为一个孩子，在妈妈偶尔遇到其他爱说闲话的人聊个没完没了时，我挺高兴的。但是，只有经常出差的爸爸不在家时才这样。有一次，爸爸突然回到家，因为有人向爸爸抱怨妈妈了。'你就不能闭

① counselor
/ˈkaʊnsələ/
n. 顾问

② boycott
/ˈbɔɪkət/
v. 排斥

③ hysterically
/hɪsˈterɪkəlɪ/
adv. 歇斯底里地

her decorum[4] for too long. It is the same with me now. "

"You see sir, my daughter has changed schools so often and this is the last school left. I told my husband that the schools were not up-to-date in their teaching methods. He is too busy with his work so he lets me do as I like."

"Ah ha, so it was your mother who taught you to gossip?"

"She did not really teach me how to gossip but it somehow came naturally. I have turned to be exactly like my mother."

"Does your daughter like to gossip?" the counselor asked.

"You know girls these days, they never want to open up to their mothers. They prefer to confide with their school peers. My daughter is a good girl and she has some friends but now they have left her. I really want to see my girl happy."

"Alright, this is what you must do and take your daughter along with you. Go to the market and buy a chicken. She must do exactly as you do. On your way back home, pluck the fine feathers of the chicken and throw them on the street as you both walk along. After you both have performed what I ordered, then come here with your daughter."

The rich lady did as the counselor asked her to do. She later returned with her daughter and said that they had faithfully[5] followed his orders.

上嘴巴吗？如果我们的女儿也学你的样子，谁还敢娶她呢？'但妈妈那高雅的举止没多久就又不见了。现在，我也是这个样子。"

"你知道，先生，我女儿已经换了好几个学校，刚刚又转了学。我告诉我丈夫说这些学校的教学方法不够先进。他工作太忙，因此，任我怎么喜欢就怎么做。"

"啊，这么说是你妈妈教你说闲话的了？"

"她没有真正教我如何说闲话，不知道怎么回事，自然而然就会了。我变得和我妈妈一模一样了。"

"你女儿喜欢说闲话吗？"顾问问道。

"当今的女孩们，你是知道的，她们从不对妈妈敞开心扉，她们更喜欢向同学倾吐心声。我女儿是个好孩子，也有一些朋友，但现在他们都离开了她。我真的想看到我女儿高高兴兴的。"

"好吧，你必须照我说的去做：带你女儿一起去市场买只鸡，你做什么就让她跟着你做什么。你们在回家的路上一边走一边拔下鸡毛扔在街上。你们两个都按我说的做过之后，再带你的女儿到我这儿来。"

这位贵夫人按照顾问所说的做了。然后，她与女儿一起回来，说她们完全遵照他的要求做了。

4 decorum
/dɪˈkɔːrəm/
n. 高雅的举止

5 faithfully
/ˈfeɪθfʊli/
adv. 忠实地，正确地

"Very good! Now please go to the market and walk along the street again and try to pick up the fine feathers which you both threw yesterday."

"That's impossible," the daughter replied. "The wind has already blown them in all directions. How can we collect the feathers again?"

"You see, your daughter is a clever girl. She read the meaning well. But don't blame the wind, lady! You gossipers always blame someone else even after you have done the damage. The same happens when you gossip about others. Your words are passed from mouth to mouth and it's impossible to stop the evil spreading once it has started. The best thing you can do is not to start. This is all I can advise you. You must think what you have to do to redeem[4] your good name."

"It is hard for me but for my daughter's sake, I will go and apologize to those parents I was so rude to. I hope they will forgive me. Most importantly, I will stop gossiping and control my tongue."

"Mama you will do this for me?" her daughter asked.

"Sure I will, girl, I want you to be happy. I am sorry to put you in this situation, girl."

"I must admit I was ashamed of you. Now, I am really proud you are my mother," as daughter and mother embraced each other.

"很好！现在，请到市场去，仍沿着那条路走，把你们两个昨天扔掉的鸡毛再捡起来。"

"这不可能，"女儿说，"风已经把鸡毛刮得到处都是了。我们怎么捡得回来呢？"

"你看，你女儿是个聪明的孩子，她领会了其中的含义。但是，不要责怪风，夫人！你们爱讲闲话的人总是责怪别人，即使损失是自己造成的。说别人闲话时也是这样。你的话从一张嘴传到另一张嘴里，一旦开始，就很难制止这种可恶的传播。你能做的最好的事就是不说。这就是我能给你的所有建议。你必须考虑该做点什么来赎回你的好名声。"

"这对我来说太难了，但是，为了我女儿，我会去向我曾经粗鲁地对待过的家长们道歉，希望他们会原谅我。最重要的是，我会管住我的舌头，不再说闲话。"

"妈妈，你会为了我而这样做吗？"她的女儿问。

"我当然会，孩子，我想让你快乐。让你陷入这种境地，我感到很难过，孩子。"

"我必须承认，我曾为你感到羞耻。现在，你是我的妈妈，我真的很自豪。"说着，母女俩拥抱在一起。

6 redeem

/rɪˈdiːm/

v. 赎回

Chinese Cinderella

中国的灰姑娘

The King was madly in love and he married Yeh Hsien and took her off to his island kingdom.

国王疯狂地爱上了叶欣，于是娶她为妻，带她去了自己的岛国。

The Cinderella story of German version tells about a poor orphan girl who was ill treated by her step-mother and her two step-sisters.

This Cinderella, the Chinese version, was the earliest known story written in the world. The story took place a long time ago, There lived a chief of a mountain cave who was called Chief Wu. He married two women, one of whom died leaving him with a baby named Yeh Hsien. She was a very intelligent girl and good at working on gold and her father loved her very much. But when he died she was mistreated[1] by her step-mother. Yeh Hsien was made to cut wood and was sent to dangerous places to draw water from deep wells.

One day, Yeh Hsien caught a fish of more than two inches long with beautiful red fins and golden eyes. She brought it home and placed it in a basin of water. Though Yeh Hsien had little to eat she often went hungry so that she could feed the fish. Every day it grew larger and larger until finally the bowl couldn't hold it at all. She had no alternative[2] but to place it in a pond.

Yeh Hsien would visit the pond daily and it would climb up to the surface and pillow its head on the bank. She would then talk to the fish like a friend. But when anyone else came, the fish would never appear. Yeh Hsien's strange behaviour was noticed by the step-mother. One day she followed Yeh Hsien and was shocked to see her step-daughter talking to the beautiful fish. The step-mother came secretly to the pond and in spite of her pleading, the fish never came out.

德国版的"灰姑娘"讲述了一个可怜的女孩被其继母和继母的女儿们虐待的故事。

这个"灰姑娘"的故事是中国版的，是全世界最早的有记载的故事。故事发生在很久以前，有一个名叫吴头领的山洞首领娶了两个女人，其中一个已经去世，给他留下一个孩子，唤作叶欣。叶欣是个非常聪明的女孩，擅长金器加工，父亲对她宠爱有加。但是，父亲死后，继母常常虐待她，让她劈柴，派她到危险的地方去从深井里提水。

有一天，叶欣抓到了一条三寸来长的鱼。鱼长着漂亮的鳍和金色的眼睛。她把鱼带回家，放在了水盆里。尽管叶欣没有多少吃的，但她宁愿自己饿着肚子，也要给鱼吃。鱼一天天长大，最后，碗里根本盛不下它了。她别无选择，只好把它放到池塘里去。

叶欣每天都要到池鱼塘去，鱼也会游到水面上，头靠在池塘边上，而她则会像对朋友一样和鱼说话。但是，其他人来的时候，鱼却不会出现。继母注意到了叶欣的古怪行为。有一天，她尾随着叶欣，当看到她的继女在和一条美丽的鱼说话时，她震惊了。这位继母悄悄来到池塘边，但无论她怎样恳求，鱼也没有出现。

❶ mistreat
/ˌmɪsˈtriːt/
v. 虐待
❷ alternative
/ɔːlˈtɜːnətɪv/
n. 选择

She resorted[3] to a ruse[4] and spoke kindly to Yeh Hsien. "I am sad to see your jacket is so tattered and torn. I will sew a new one for you so let me have this old one as a sample." When the new jacket was done and in order not to cause any suspicion, she sent Yeh Hsien to fetch water miles away.

The step-mother then put on Yeh Hsien's old jacket and with a knife in her sleeve went to the pond. She called out to the fish and as it recognized the jacket, it put its head out of the water. The step-mother quickly caught hold of the fish and killed it. The fish was by then over ten feet long. The step-mother cooked the fish which tasted many times sweeter than any other fish she had eaten. She then buried its bones in a dunghill.

The next day when Yeh Hsien came home, she approached the pond only to find that the fish had vanished[5]. The poor girl went into the woods and wept her heart out. A man with disheveled hair and in a ragged garment descended from the sky and comforted her. "Do not cry, girl. Your step-mother has killed the fish and its bones are buried under a dunghill. Go home and carry the bones to your room and hide them. Whatever you shall want, pray to it and your wish will be granted." Yeh Hsien followed his advice and it was not long after that she had gold, jewels and finery of such costly texture to delight any woman's heart.

Every year, the natives of the cave mountain would organize a festival. Yeh Hsien was not allowed to attend but was told to stay home and watch the fruit orchard. She watched her step-mother

她要用一个计谋，就和善地对叶欣说："你的上衣都穿得这么破烂了，我看了心里真难受。我要给你做一件新的，把这件旧的给我做样子吧。"新衣服做好之后，为了不引起怀疑，她派叶欣到几里外的地方去提水。

于是，继母穿上叶欣的衣服，袖子里揣着一把刀向池塘走去。她呼喊着鱼，当鱼认出了衣服时，把头露出了水面。继母迅速抓住了鱼，把它杀死了。当时，这条鱼已经有一尺来长了。继母把鱼煮着吃了，这条鱼吃起来比她吃过的所有的鱼都香好多倍。她把鱼骨头埋在了粪堆里。

第二天，叶欣回到家后去池塘，却发现鱼已经不见了。可怜的女孩跑到树林里，哭得心都碎了。一位头发凌乱、衣衫褴褛的男子从天而降来安慰她，"别哭了，姑娘，你的继母把鱼杀死了，骨头埋在粪堆里。回家去把骨头拿到你房间里藏起来。无论你想要什么，只要你向它祈祷，你的愿望就会实现的。"叶欣按他的忠告去做了，很快，她就有了黄金、珠宝、以及昂贵的布料做成的华丽的衣服，这些东西能让任何一个女人高兴起来。

每年，村民们都会举行一次山洞宴会。叶欣不允许参加，只能待在家里看守果园。

❸ resort
/rɪˈzɔːt/
v. 诉诸

❹ ruse
/ˈruːs/
n. 诡计

❺ vanish
/ˈvænɪʃ/
v. 消失

and her step-sister dressed in fine clothes hurrying to the festival. After they had gone some distance away, Yeh Hsien arrayed herself in the most beautiful green silk jacket and went to the festival. The step-sister's sharp eyes noticed that the girl in the green silk jacket was none other than Yeh Hsien. "Mother how could she be here?" The step-mother too recognized it was Yeh Hsien. When the poor girl became aware of the sly glances of her step-mother and her step-sister, she ran away in a hurry and one of her slippers slipped off her foot. It was then handed into the hands of the cave people.

When mother and daughter came home, Yeh Hsien was found sleeping with her arms around the tree, so the step-mother put aside her thoughts about the identity of the girl in the green silk jacket.

Near the cave was an island kingdom called T'o Huan. The King had a strong army and he ruled over a couple of dozen islands and all its territorial waters said to cover several thousand li. One cave man who got the slipper sold it to the T'o Huan Kingdom, which finally found its way to the King. It was such a beautiful slipper that the King made all the women in his palace to try it on. The slipper was either too long or an inch too short for those even with small feet. The King was furious and suspected that the cave man got the slipper from dubious[6] sources. The man was imprisoned and tortured[7]. But he could not tell where the slipper came from.

她眼看着继母和继母的女儿穿着漂亮的衣服匆匆赶往宴会。等她们走远之后，叶欣穿上漂亮的绿丝衣去参加宴会。继母的女儿犀利的眼睛注意到，身穿绿丝衣的女孩不是别人，正是叶欣。"妈妈，她怎么会在这儿？"继母也认出了叶欣。可怜的女孩注意到继母和继母的女儿那狡诈的眼神时，匆忙逃跑了，一只鞋从脚上滑落了下来。后来，这只鞋被传到了穴居人的手中。

母亲和女儿回到家时，看到叶欣抱着树睡着了，因此，继母也就不再想弄清穿绿丝衣女孩身份的事。

山洞旁边是一个叫图奂国的岛国。国王拥有一支强大的军队，统治着几十个岛屿，据说其水域绵延数千里。有一位穴居人得到那只鞋后把它卖到了图奂国，最后到了国王手中。这只鞋非常漂亮，国王让宫里所有的女人试穿了这只鞋，但它太小了，即使是脚最小的女人穿也还是小一寸。国王勃然大怒，怀疑这只鞋是那个穴居人从什么可疑的地方弄来的。那个人被关进了监狱，严刑拷打，但他却说不出鞋是从哪里来的。

最后，国王派信使挨家挨户去查，穴居人家的女孩都穿了那只鞋，还是没有一个合适的。到叶欣家的时候，她静静地穿上了

❻ **dubious**
/ˈdjuːbɪəs/
adj. 可疑的

❼ **torture**
/ˈtɔːtʃə/
v. 用刑

Finally the King sent his couriers[8] to the every household in the cave mountain and the girls were made to put it on. Again none could fit it. When it came to Yeh Hsien's house, the girl quietly put on the slipper and it fitted her exactly. Then Yeh Hsien went into her room, quickly dressed herself in the silk green jacket and had the couriers surprised. She marched out gracefully with the other slipper on her feet. A report was made to the King who came personally to see Yeh Hsien who looked like a goddess. The King was madly in love and he married Yeh Hsien and took her off to his island kingdom.

The King and his queen Yeh Hsien lived happily for some years until he discovered Yeh Hsien' fish bones. He became greedy and kept asking for more and more gold. Later, when he found that the bones could not give him what he wanted anymore, the King took the bones and threw them into the sea. Where the bones went to no one knew. The King also disappeared and no one knew his whereabouts too.

Yeh Hsien then ruled the island kingdom justly for many years. As for her step-mother and step-sister, she forgave them and whenever they visited her, both women were well treated.

Moral: To forgive is divine!

鞋，正合适。于是，叶欣到自己的房间去迅速穿上了那身绿丝衣，令信使们惊讶不已。她穿上另一只鞋，迈起了优雅的步伐。信使向国王报告之后，国王亲自来见女神一般的叶欣。国王疯狂地爱上了叶欣，于是娶她为妻，带她去了自己的岛国。

国王和叶欣王后过了大概一年的幸福生活，但国王发现叶欣的鱼骨头之后，变得非常贪婪，不断地要越来越多的金子。后来，当国王发现鱼骨头再也不能给他所要的东西时，便拿起鱼骨头，把它们扔进了大海。鱼骨头哪里去了，谁也不知道。国王也消失了。他去了哪里，也没有人知道。

此后的多年里，叶欣公正地治理着这个岛国。至于她的继母和继母的女儿，叶欣原谅了她们。每当两个女人来看她时，都会受到很好的招待。

寓意：原谅是神圣的！

❽ courier
/ˈkʊrɪə/
v. 信使

Adventures of Tiny, the tiniest, ugliest mouse in the world

小丑鼠"小不点儿"历险记

But I was called Tiny, the tiniest, ugliest mouse that ever lived.

但是，人们都叫我小不点儿，世界上最小、最丑的老鼠。

"Papa is here, hurrah!" "How are my two little darlings? Have you two been good and not fight with each other?" he asked. "We've been very good, papa," the twins chorused.[1] "Papa, you promised to tell us why your name is Tiny!" "Okay, come and lie on my lap and papa will tell you why!" This was the story he told them.

I was born the tiniest, ugliest mouse the world had ever seen. Because of my size and a mole[2] that grew over my left eye it made me looked as if I was blinded in one eye. I would stumble[3] and fall easily. "He's so different from his sister, she's so pretty," mama would say to papa. "Liza, let me carry him." So dear papa would carry me on his back and played with me. Wherever papa went, I followed. "Don't be angry with your mama, Tiny, that's what he called me, I am sure inside her heart, and you're still her child." I was not worried as I had papa's love. But one day, while papa was hunting for food, a big fat cat came from nowhere and put its claws on papa's eye. Papa groaned with pain. When mama saw what had happened, she shouted at me and said, "see what you've done to your papa, isn't it enough to have one blind mouse, now I will have two. You bring us nothing but trouble." That night I was naturally sad. I was not allowed to see papa so I ran away.

The journey was tough. I could not get enough food or water to drink. Everyone I met avoided me. Some even hurled stones and cursed me, "Get out of our sight!" When I finally reached a farm, I saw a cow. A little distance away, was a chicken feeding her little

"好哇！爸爸回来啦！""我的两个小宝贝，你们好吗？乖不乖啊？没有打架吧？"他问道。"我们很乖，爸爸。"这对双胞胎齐声说。"爸爸，你答应过要告诉我们你为什么叫小不点儿的！""好吧，过来坐到我腿上，爸爸来告诉你们为什么！"下面就是他给他们讲的故事。

我生来就是世界上最小、最丑的老鼠。由于我个子小，左眼上还有一颗黑痣，看起来像瞎了一只眼睛。我走路摇摇晃晃，很容易摔倒。"他和他姐姐可真不一样，她多漂亮。"妈妈会对爸爸说。"丽莎，让我来抱抱他吧。"亲爱的爸爸会把我背在背上和我玩耍。爸爸去哪儿我都跟着。"不要生你妈妈的气，小不点儿(他是那样叫我的)，我相信，在她心中你依然是她的孩子。"我并不担心，因为我有爸爸的爱。但是，有一天，爸爸猎食时，不知从哪儿来了一只大肥猫抓伤了爸爸的眼睛。爸爸痛苦地呻吟着。当妈妈看到发生的一切时，对我大喊道："看看你对你爸爸都做了什么？有一只瞎眼的老鼠还不够吗？现在要有两只了，你只会给我们带来麻烦。"那天晚上，我自然是很伤心。他们不许我见爸爸，所以我就离家出走了。

这段旅程很艰辛。我找不到足够的食物和水，遇到的每个人都躲着我，有些人甚至还朝我扔石头，并骂我"滚开，别让我看见！"最

❶ chorus

/ˈkɔːrəs/

v. 齐声说

❷ mole

/məʊl/

n. 痣

❸ stumble

/ˈstʌmbl/

v. 走路摇晃

chicks. I was hungry and needed some rest. The chicken flapped[4] out her feathers and ran to protect her chicks. The cow cried "moo, moo" — "go away you ugly creature!" I was too weak to answer. "Where on earth did you come from?" the chicken asked. "I've ... walked a long way..." I answered. "Can I rest here as I am very tired." One little innocent chick that broke loose came running and licked me all over. "She must have taken a fancy to you," the mother chicken said. "Alright, you go and rest at the far end of the barn. If the farmer and his wife see you, they will not be happy." So I slept at the far end of the barn behind some poles.

The next morning, the farmer came to milk the cow and his fat wife threw some grains for the chicken and her chicks. After they left, I was told that I could eat the left-over crusts with hardly any grains inside and licked the split milk on the ground. "Thank you, I'm grateful for your kindness."

A few days later, the cow and the chicken said, "It's time for you to repay our kindness." The plan was for me to enter the farmer's house and look for some chocolates for them to eat. "We know the farmer's wife loved chocolates. We cannot enter the house but you are so tiny, no one would see you."

That night, I crept into the kitchen and found no one was there. The cupboard was filled with rows and rows of chocolates. I squeaked[5] and danced with joy when my face hit against a big mirror. It was the first time I saw my image. The tiniest, ugliest mouse that ever lived. No wonder everyone avoided me. Some pieces of

后，我来到了一个农场，看到一头奶牛，不远处还有一只正在喂小鸡的母鸡。我很饿，还需要休息。母鸡张开翅膀保护小鸡，奶牛"哞——哞"地叫着"——走开，丑陋的家伙！"我太虚弱了，没有力气答话。"你到底是从哪儿来的？"母鸡问。"我已经……走了很长一段路……"我回答，"我太累了，能不能在这里休息一会儿？"一只纯真的小鸡打破了僵局，跑过来舔我的全身。"她一定是喜欢上你了，"鸡妈妈说，"好吧，你到粮仓那一头去休息吧，如果农夫和他妻子看见你，会不高兴的。"所以，我就在粮仓的那一头的几根柱子后面睡下了。

第二天早上，农夫进来挤牛奶，他的胖妻子给鸡妈妈的小鸡撒点儿粮食。他们离开之后，母鸡和奶牛说我可以吃几乎没剩下什么粮食的谷壳，舔舔洒在地上的牛奶。"谢谢你们，我很感激你们的好意。"

几天之后，奶牛和母鸡说："现在是你回报我们的好意的时候了。"计划是由我到农夫的房里去给他们找些巧克力吃。"我们知道农夫的妻子喜欢吃巧克力。我们进不去房子，但是，你这么小，没有人会看到你的。"

那天夜里，我悄悄爬进厨房，发现里面没人。托盘上放着一排排的巧克力。我高兴得又唱又跳，突然，我的脸撞到了一面镜子上。这

❹ flap
/flæp/
v. 拍动，拍打
❺ squeak
/skwiːk/
v. 发出尖叫

half-eaten chocolates were thrown on the floor. I picked up two pieces, one for the cow and a slighter bigger piece for the chicken as she had her chicks to feed.

The cow and the chicken enjoyed the chocolates very much. Not a tiny bite was offered me. Again, bless the little chick. She placed her tiny mouth against mine to give me a taste of the chocolate. "I don't know why she likes you," the chicken said angrily "Well, we want only chocolates," the cow and the chicken reminded me. "Don't bring us anything else." Knowing how selfish my friends were, I always took a bite of the chocolate first before I left the kitchen.

One night, as I was about to enter the kitchen, I heard the farmer saying "Wife, do you notice we have been losing some chocolates lately. I went to town and bought a trap[6]." It was a mousetrap. I hurriedly left and told the chicken and the cow about the trap. I apologized for not bringing any chocolates for them. Instead of sympathizing[7] with me, they were terribly annoyed. "Why don't you wait until the kitchen is clear, you silly ugly mouse?" "I was afraid," I answered. "So you saw a mouse trap, what has that got to do with us? You know, we give eggs and milk so the farmer and his wife would not harm us. Don't forget your promise to bring us a piece of chocolate every night as long as you live with us." I had no alternative but to fulfill my "chocolate" mission.

The following night, the farmer had laid the trap door open. As the spring in the trap snapped, it gave out a loud bang. The farmer and his wife came to see what was happening. A snake

是我第一次看见自己的样子,世界上最小、最
丑的老鼠,难怪谁都躲着我。几块吃了一半的
巧克力被扔在了地板上。我捡了两块,一块给
奶牛,稍大的一块给母鸡,因为她得喂小鸡。

奶牛和母鸡非常喜欢这些巧克力,而我却
连一小口都没有吃到。还要再一次感谢那只小
鸡,她把自己的小嘴贴到我的嘴上让我尝了尝
巧克力的味道。"我真不知道她为什么会喜欢
你。"母鸡生气地说。"好啦,我们只想要巧克
力,"奶牛和母鸡提醒我说,"别给我们带来任何
别的东西。"知道我的朋友们多么自私之后,我
总是在离开厨房之前先咬一口巧克力。

一天夜里,正当我要进入厨房时,听到农
夫说:"老婆,你有没有注意到最近我们丢了一
些巧克力?我去镇上买了一个夹子。"那是一个
老鼠夹。我赶忙离开,把老鼠夹的事告诉了母
鸡和奶牛。我为未能给他们带来巧克力而道歉,
他们不但没有同情我,还恼羞成怒。"为什么你
不等到厨房里没有人了呢,你这个傻瓜丑老
鼠?""我害怕。"我回答。"你看见老鼠夹与我们
有什么关系?你知道,我们下蛋、产奶,农夫和他
妻子是不会伤害我们的。别忘了,你答应只要和
我们住在一起,就要每天晚上给我们弄一块巧
克力来。"我别无选择,只能去执行我的"巧克
力"任务。

6 **trap**
/træp/
n. 夹子
7 **sympathize**
/ˈsɪmpəθaɪz/
v. 同情

was caught inside it. The twisted spring wire in the trap had knocked the snake's head and it died immediately.

"Husband, I was told the snake's flesh is very tender. It will also cure my high blood pressure," the fat wife said. So she brewed the snake with all kind of herbs[8] in a big pot of hot boiling water. "I never knew snake meat tasted so good," she later boasted to her neighbor.

Not long after, the fat wife fell ill with high temperature. The farmer called the neighbor for help. "Your wife had added too many herbs for such a small baby snake, " she said, "the concoction[9] may have been too strong for her." Everyone in the village knew how greedy his fat wife was.

"Why don't I boil chicken soup for her," the neighbor suggested, "this will cool down your wife's temperature." In fact this neighbor was eyeing the chicken for a long while and this was her chance to get a share of the chicken soup. "Please do what you think is best for her," cried the farmer.

The neighbor quickly grabbed hold of the chicken and before it could flapped its feathers, slaughtered it into chicken soup. "Drink this chicken soup, my friend, and you'll be up and about in no time," the sly neighbor said to the farmer's wife as he stood watching. Instead of getting cured, the poor fat wife became seriously ill. The farmer called for his son who lived in town to come. When the man came, he was so angry. "I told you to sell off the farm. Come

第二天夜里，农夫把老鼠夹的开关打开了。夹子上的弹簧收缩时发出了很响的嘣的一声。农夫和妻子来看是怎么回事。是一条蛇被夹住了。缠在夹子上的弹簧线打在了蛇的头上，蛇当时就死了。

"老公，我听说蛇肉非常鲜嫩，还可以治好我的高血压。"胖妻子说。她用一大锅滚开的水炖了这条蛇，还加了各种调味的药草。"我以前从不知道蛇肉这么好吃。"她后来向邻居炫耀说。

此后不久，胖妻子发高烧病倒了。农夫叫邻居来帮忙。"你妻子炖那么小的蛇却放了那么多的药草，"她说，"蛇汤对她来说可能太浓烈了。"村子里每个人都知道他的胖妻子有多么贪婪。

"为什么不给你妻子熬点儿鸡汤喝呢？"邻居建议说，"那会使她退烧的。"事实上，这位邻居已经觊觎这只鸡很久了，这是她分一点儿鸡汤喝的机会。"你觉得什么对她有好处就做什么吧。"农夫哭着说。

这位邻居迅速逮住了母鸡，在她还没来得及扑愣翅膀之前就把她宰了熬汤了。"把鸡汤喝了吧，你马上就会好起来的。"农夫站在一旁看时，狡猾的邻居对他的妻子说。可怜的胖妻子的病不但没有治好，反而更加严重了。

8 herb

/hɜːb/

n. 药草

9 concoction

/kənˈkɒkʃən/

n. 混合物

and live with me but you still want to stick in this dirty farm. You both are stubborn."

The farmer and his fat wife had no choice but to abandon their farm. Before the couple left, their son said, "I will return and clear up the place and get an agent to sell off the property. We can't keep the cow so she will also have to go! "

I was terribly saddened. Though the cow and the chicken had been unkind, they took me in and I felt I would miss them. The neighbor took the motherless chicks and the cow was soon sold to another farmer.

In the meantime, I had the whole place to myself. As I was examining what I should do with the mousetrap, I heard a lovely squeak and before me stood the prettiest little mouse I had ever seen. "I have been hiding in the hole in the kitchen and was observing all that you have done for the cow and the chicken. Don't be afraid of the trap. If only we could pull off the spring wire loose, then it will no longer be a danger to us. I will help you." After some hard pulling, we managed to get the wire loosened. She congratulated me and said her name was Jeanie.

"How pretty and clever you're, Jeanie," I exclaimed. "Well, if I may return your compliment[10], you are the biggest and kindest mouse I've ever seen." "But I was called Tiny, the tiniest, ugliest mouse that ever lived." "Go and see how you look in the mirror," Jeanie advised. I was shocked! The mirror reflected that I had grown big-

农夫打电话把住在镇上的儿子叫来了。他回来之后非常生气。"我告诉过你们把农场卖掉，过来和我一起住，但是你们就是想住在这个脏兮兮的农场里。你们两个太固执了。"

农夫和妻子别无选择，只好放弃农场。在这对夫妇离开之前，他们的儿子说："我会回来清理这个地方的，再找个代理人把这块地卖掉。我们不能留着奶牛，所以她也得走！"

我感到非常难过。尽管奶牛和母鸡一直很不友善，但他们接纳了我，我想我会想念他们的。那个邻居带走了失去妈妈的小鸡，没多久，奶牛也被卖给了另一个农夫。

在这段时间里，整个农场都是我一个人的。在我检查应该怎样处理老鼠夹时，听到一声欢快的鼠叫，在我面前站着一只我平生所见过的最漂亮的小老鼠。"我一直藏在厨房里的这个洞里，看着你为奶牛和母鸡所做的一切。别害怕老鼠夹，只要我们能够把弹簧线拉松，它对我们就不再是威胁了。我来帮你。"一番费力的拉拽之后，我们成功地把线松开了。她向我道贺，并说她的名字叫詹妮。

"你真漂亮、真聪明，詹妮！"我惊叫着说。"那么，如果要我回报你的称赞的话，你是我见过的最大、最善良的老鼠。""但是，人们都叫我小不点儿，世界上最小、最丑的老鼠。"

❿ **compliment**
/ˈkɒmplimənt/
n. 恭维

ger and the mole no longer covered my eye. In fact, I had turned into quite a good-looking mouse. "The chocolates had nourished[11] you well," Jeanie murmured sweetly.

Jeanie and I were soon married. I told her about my mama and papa and why I ran away from home. "Tiny, don't you like to see your mama and papa again? We could use the trap, fill it up with chocolates and take them home. The farm will soon have a new owner, so it's best we get away from here," your mama suggested. I was worried if my mama still hated me. "Don't be silly, you're still her flesh and blood! I'm sure when she sees you, there will be a happy reunion." your mama reassured[12] me.

When we reached home, I cried out, "Mama, papa." Everyone came running out and dear papa whose eyesight was not too good, cried out, "Is this my Tiny, tell me I'm not dreaming. Are you really my Tiny I used to carry on my back? What a good looking mouse I see!" "Yes, papa I'm Tiny." Then I introduced your mama and said, "Papa, mama, this is my dearest wife, Jeanie, we both have come home. We bought a lot of chocolates too." While they were enjoying the chocolates, mama and papa asked so many questions. How I survived, how I met your mama, how I was transformed from the tiniest, ugliest mouse into such a big and good-looking mouse. They were never tired to hear my adventures in a far away farm where I met your mama. Your grandma apologized for the way she treated me. "We are family and all's well that ends well," I replied.

"去照照镜子,看看自己的样子吧。"詹妮建议。我震惊了! 镜子里的我已经长大了,盖在左眼上的痣也不见了。事实上,我已经变成了一只非常帅气的老鼠。"是巧克力滋养了你,"詹妮甜甜地低声说道。

我和詹妮结了婚。我告诉她有关我父母以及我为何离家出走的事。"小不点儿,难道你不想再见到你的爸爸妈妈吗? 我们可以利用这个老鼠夹,把它装满巧克力带回家。不久,这个农场就会有个新主人,所以我们最好离开这儿。"你们的妈妈建议说。我担心妈妈是否依然讨厌我。"别傻了,你到底也是她的骨肉啊! 我相信,你们相见时,一定是一场愉快的团聚。"你们的妈妈这样安慰我说。

我们到家的时候,我喊道:"妈妈,爸爸。"大家都跑了出来,视力不太好的亲爱的爸爸喊着:"是不是我的小不点儿? 我不是在做梦吧? 你真的是我过去常背着的小不点儿吗? 你看起来真帅气啊!""是的,爸爸,我是小不点儿。"接着,我介绍了你们的妈妈。我说:"爸爸,这是我亲爱的妻子詹妮,我们一起回家来了,还带回来好多巧克力。"妈妈和爸爸边吃巧克力边问这问那:我是怎么活下来的,如何与你们的妈妈相遇的,怎么从一只最小、最丑的老鼠变成了一只高大、帅气的老鼠的。他们

❶ nourish
/ˈnʌrɪʃ/
v. 滋养
❷ reassure
/riːəˈʃʊə/
v. 使…安心

A dinner was arranged and papa and mama's relatives and friends were invited. Someone was heard to say to papa, "So your <u>prodigal son</u>[13] has returned." "He's the best prodigal son," papa said proudly. The occasion ended with chocolates being served to all the guests present. The adventures of Tiny, the tiniest, ugliest mouse that ever lived, spread far and wide!

Our family increased. It may be a coincidence[14], your grandma gave birth to twins, your aunt and I. When it was your mama's time, she too gave birth to you twins.

"It's such a lovely story, papa," one twin said, and the other added, "what an adventure, papa," and they were soon fast asleep on their papa's lap.

Moral: Face any obstacle that may come your way bravely and you'll emerge stronger and wiser.

不知疲倦地听我讲述在与你们的妈妈相遇的那个遥远的农场里的历险故事。你们的祖母为她那样对待我而向我道歉。"我们都是一家人,只要大家都好,就一切都好。"我回答说。

爸爸妈妈安排了一次晚宴,亲戚朋友都受到了邀请。有人对爸爸说:"你的浪子回头啦!""他是最棒的浪子。"爸爸自豪地说。在晚宴的最后,我们请所有在场的客人享用巧克力。小不点儿,世界上最小、最丑的老鼠的历险记传到四面八方啦!

我们家族的人数越来越多。你们的祖母生了我和你们的姑妈一对双胞胎,到你们的妈妈的时候,她也生了你们这一对双胞胎。这可能是巧合吧。

"这个故事真好听,爸爸,"双胞胎中的一个说。另一个补充道:"多有趣的一次冒险啊,爸爸。"两兄弟很快就在爸爸的腿上进入了梦乡。

寓意:勇敢面对可能发生的任何困难,你会变得更强大、更睿智。

⓭ **prodigal son**
浪子
⓮ **coincidence**
/kəʊˈɪnsɪdəns/
n. 巧合

Simple Simon

傻瓜西蒙

I have traveled all over the globe in search of people like you.

要找一个像你这样的人，我已走遍了全世界。

Everybody in the village used to laugh at Simon. They nick-named him Simple Simon in school, as he could not retain what he had learnt. Even his mother thought he would never grow into a clever boy. She, however, loved her son very much. He grew up to be a good-looking, strong lad like his father and was very help-ful in the house. What her husband told her on his sick bed before he died never left her mind: "Wife, please take good care of our little boy. Be patient with him as you've been patient with me. I'm sorry I shall not be around to see him grow up." He was the best husband any woman could have. He had worked so hard to build up the little farm for the family. The farm stood at the crossroads to other farms and thus no travelers would miss it. Simple Simon's mother earned her income by turning one of the rooms as a rest-ing place for travelers.

"Sir, there's a room if you wish to stay," she would say. Her charges were moderate[1] and even if the visitor had no means to pay her, she would not turn him away. She would then call out to her son to take the traveler to his room.

One day an elderly, well-dressed and distinguished looking trav-eler knocked at the farm door. He had traveled far and wide and wanted a room to rest. After the man was settled in the room, Sim-ple Simon brought him a cup of hot tea and a slice of egg pud-ding. When the man took a bite of the pudding, he asked, "Who baked this egg pudding? It's the most delicious pudding I've ever tasted. It's neither too creamy nor is it soggy[2], and it melts deliciously in my mouth! What's your name, lad?" "I am called

村子里每个人都常取笑西蒙。在学校里，人们给他取绰号为"傻瓜西蒙"，因为他记不住所学的知识。甚至他的妈妈都觉得他永远也不会变成一个聪明的男孩。然而，她却非常爱他。他长成了一个像他爸爸一样帅气、强壮的小伙子，成了家里的顶梁柱。病榻上的丈夫临终前对她说的话她从未忘记过："老婆，好好照顾我们的小儿子，对他耐心点儿，就像你一直耐心地对我一样。不能在他身边看着他长大，我感到很难过。"他是天下最好的丈夫，为给这个家建立一个小农场，他曾那么辛苦地劳作。农场坐落在通往其他农场的十字路口处，因此，行人都会路过这里。傻瓜西蒙的妈妈把一间屋子改作行人歇脚的地方，赚点儿收入。

"先生，如果你想要住下来，这里有一间屋子。"她会这样说。她的收费适中，即使来者没有钱付给她，她也不会把他拒之门外。她会喊她的儿子把行人带到他自己的房间去。

一天，一位上了年纪、穿着考究、看起来很高贵的行人叩响了农场的门。他已经走过了很多地方，想找间屋子休息一下。这个人在屋子里安顿下来之后，傻瓜西蒙给他端来一杯热茶和一块鸡蛋布丁。这个人咬了一口布丁，问道："是谁烤的鸡蛋布丁？这是

① moderate
/ˈmɒdərɪt/
adj. 适中的

② soggy
/ˈsɒgɪ/
adj. 潮乎乎的

Simple Simon. Sir, mother's egg pudding is steamed[3] not baked. I'm glad you like it and I will tell her what you said," he replied proudly. "You mean the pudding was not baked?" "Oh no, Sir, I used to help mother stir the pudding for quite a long while under very low fire. Only when the pudding gets thickened, I will stop stirring. It will then turn crispy[4] and gives out a lovely-brownish-golden color."

"My! My! Your description of your mother's egg pudding makes my mouth water. Do you think I could have another slice?" Of course, Sir, it's our pleasure to serve you." Simple Simon hurriedly went to his mother and excitingly told her what the old gentleman said and wanted. He returned with another slice of the pudding and this time, with a cup of hot lemon tea. "Now, tell me why you are called Simple Simon?" the man asked. "Sir, because I am slow in learning and often forgot what I was taught in school." "Are you angry when people called you Simple Simon?" "No Sir, maybe it is for my own good." "Why?" the gentleman asked. "Because then I will not gossip[5] and cause trouble to other people." The elderly man laughed out loud and said, "Simple Simon, you're one unique boy I've ever met. Your wise answer and the loving manner you have described your mother's egg pudding have made my day. I have traveled all over the globe in search of people like you. You see, I left home and have been traveling ever since because an old gossipy neighbor would make up stories about me to my wife so much so our relationship was broken up."

The old gentleman took out from his bag some little notebooks,

我吃过的最好吃的布丁。不太油腻，也不潮乎乎的，而且入口即化，太好吃了！你叫什么名字，小伙子？""人们都叫我傻瓜西蒙，先生，妈妈的鸡蛋布丁是蒸的，不是烤的。我很高兴您喜欢吃，我会把您的话告诉妈妈的。"他骄傲地回答。"你的意思是这布丁不是烤的？""噢，是的，先生，我常帮妈妈搅拌布丁，要在文火上搅拌好长时间。直到布丁变粘稠的时候，我才停止搅拌。然后，布丁就会变脆，呈现出一种可人的、略棕的金黄色。"

"哎呦！你描述你妈妈做的鸡蛋布丁说得我直流口水。我可以再来一块吗？""当然，先生，我们很乐意为您效劳。"傻瓜西蒙赶忙跑到妈妈跟前，兴奋地告诉她老先生说的话和他想要的东西。他回来了，拿了一块布丁，还有一杯热柠檬茶。"现在告诉我，为什么人们叫你傻瓜西蒙？"这个人问。"先生，因为我学东西很慢，经常会忘记在学校里老师教的知识。""人们叫你傻瓜西蒙时，你生气吗？""不，先生，可能那是为了我自己好吧。""为什么？"这位先生问。"因为那样我就不会说长道短，给别人添麻烦了。"老人爽朗地笑了，说："傻瓜西蒙，你是我见过的最独特的孩子。你睿智的

❸ **steam**
/stiːm/
v. 蒸
❹ **crispy**
/ˈkrɪspɪ/
adj. 脆的
❺ **gossip**
/ˈɡɒsɪp/
v. 说闲话

a packet filled with pens and pencils and handed them to Simple Simon, and "I'm really touched by your simplicity. I was once a teacher and now I write books for children and adults." He showed Simple Simon a thick writing pad filled with written notes. "Each time I visit a place and find anything interesting I will write what I see. Can I give you a little advice, lad? "

"Of course, kind Sir! " replied Simple Simon eagerly.

"Alright, Simple Simon, whenever you think you will forget what you have been taught, <u>jot them down</u>[6] in your notebook. You may have to go over what you have written several times so be patient. I bet your brain will keep on ticking and you'll be a genius in no time."

"Sir, thank you for your suggestion. I only want to make mother happy as she worked so hard to look after the farm and me. Even when people called me 'stupid' mother would say, 'Son, I always pray to your father to help us. He was a good and kind man. You also pray and ask your father to help you and I am sure things will change for the better some day.' "

When the old man heard that Simon's father died when he was only two years old, he took the boy's hands and petted his head. Soon the two were chatting and exchanging views with each other all night long.

回答和描述你妈妈做的鸡蛋布丁时的样子令
我非常高兴。要找一个像你这样的人，我已
走遍了全世界。你知道，我离开家之后，一
直在旅行，因为一个好说闲话的老邻居编派
我的故事对我妻子讲，以致于我们的关系都
破裂了。"

　　这位老先生从他的包里拿出一些小笔记
本和一个装满钢笔、铅笔的盒子，并把这些
东西递给了傻瓜西蒙，"你的纯朴深深打动
了我。我曾是一名教师，现在写一些给孩子
和成人看的书。"他给傻瓜西蒙看一本写满
了笔记的厚厚的拍纸簿。"我每到一个地
方，发现有趣的事情，就写下来。我可以给
你点儿建议吗，小伙子？"

　　"当然，好心的先生！"傻瓜西蒙急切地
回答。

　　"那好，傻瓜西蒙，每当你认为你会忘
记老师教的知识时，就把它们记在笔记本
上。可能你要反复看上几遍所写下的内容，
所以，耐心点儿。我打赌你的大脑会不断转
动，很快你就会成为一个天才。"

　　"先生，谢谢您的建议，我只想让妈妈
高兴。为了照顾我和农场，她干活太辛苦
了。即使人们叫我傻瓜时，她也会说：'儿
子，我一直向你爸爸祈祷，让他帮助我们。

⑥ jot down
记下

The next day before the old gentleman bade Simple Simon and his mother goodbye, Simple Simon said, "Sir, I would like to be a teacher like you some day. I hope to write all I learnt to bene-fit others." The old gentleman laughingly replied, "Not gossip, Simple Simon! " "Yes, Sir, no gossip for me! " Turning to Simon's mother, he added, "Madam, thank you for your hospitality and your egg pudding is fit for a king! It's simply delicious. There's a saying, 'once tasted always wanted' and if I stayed here longer I would love to have your egg pudding everyday. Your boy is unique! "

Not long after, Simple Simon became the cleverest boy in school. He won the first prize when he entered the school's essay contest entitled "Mama's Egg Pudding". He wrote vividly about the old gentleman who loved his mother's egg pudding and who had encouraged him. Now he always carries a notebook in his shirt pocket. Any classmates who asked him for help were not turned away even though they had made fun of his name and called "stupid." Several times he was asked if he would like to change his name to "Clever Simon." "I shall remain a simple person and Simple Simon suits me. My name is my lucky mascot[7]."

Simple Simon later became a teacher in the village school and was often heard telling his students, "Always look what's written inside a book and don't judge it by its cover! "

Whenever mother and son were free, they would visit Simple Simon's father gravesite. Both bought flowers to lay on the tomb

他是一个善良的好人。你也祈祷，让你爸爸帮助你，我相信将来有一天情况会好起来的。'"

当老人听说在西蒙两岁时爸爸就去世了时，他拉起西蒙的手，抚摸着他的头。很快，两个人就攀谈起来，并倾心交谈了整个晚上。

第二天，在老先生与傻瓜西蒙和他妈妈道别之前，傻瓜西蒙说："先生，我希望有一天我能成为一名像您一样的教师。我希望能把所学的全写出来造福他人。"老先生笑着说："不要说长道短，傻瓜西蒙！""好的，先生，我决不会说长道短！"老先生又转向西蒙的妈妈，说："夫人，谢谢您的款待，您做的鸡蛋布丁都可以献给国王了！真是太好吃了。有句话说：'偶尝一次，唇齿留香。'如果我在这里多待一段时间，我愿每天都吃到您做的鸡蛋布丁。您的儿子是独一无二的！"

不久以后，傻瓜西蒙成了学校里最聪明的孩子。他报名参加了学校的作文竞赛，得了一等奖，作文的题目为《妈妈的鸡蛋布丁》。他惟妙惟肖地描绘了那位爱吃他妈妈做的鸡蛋布丁并鼓励他的老先生。现在，他总是在衬衫口袋里装着一个笔记本。任何向他求助的同学，哪怕是曾拿他的名字取乐、

❼ **mascot**
/ˈmæskət/
n. 吉祥物

stone as they prayed for they knew he was watching over them,
"Husband, you will be happy to see how well your son has turned
out to be." When it was Simple Simon's turn to pray he said,
"Thank you father, did you send the wise old gentleman to guide
me." "Your father sent you a Guardian Angel," his mother replied
as tears rolled down her eyes. After they had finished their prayers,
mother and son would walk home hand in hand, their hearts at
peace.

Simple Simon was very devoted[8] to his mother. As she was
getting older, she decided to invite her young widowed sister named
Bessie to live with them. To supplement the household income further, Simple Simon's mother and aunt Bessie were busy steaming
egg puddings for sale. "It's your grandmother's secret recipe," his
mother and aunt Bessie would tell Simple Simon. Though his mother never complained, he knew her health was not so good as she
was getting rather weak.

One day aunt Bessie took Simple Simon aside and told him
that his mother suffered from a weak heart. "She was a good mother
and you have been a good son but be prepared that she may not
live too long. Don't be sad as I will do all I can for her." His mother's death came suddenly as one night she had a heart attack.
Simple Simon was devastated[9] and refused to eat for a couple of
days. "Your mother would not be happy if you continue this way.
We both knew you would like to travel. Now it is the time. See how
other people live and learn their culture. I'll look after the farm
and continue to steam your grandma's egg pudding!" aunt Bessie

叫他傻瓜的同学，他都不会拒绝。有几次，
有人问他是否想把名字改为"聪明的西蒙"。
他回答说："我还是个普通人，普通的西蒙
（原文 Simple 为多义词，其中有傻瓜、普通
之意）挺适合我。我的名字是给我带来幸运
的吉祥物。"

后来，傻瓜西蒙成了乡村学校的教师，
经常有人听到他告诫他的学生说："不要从
封面来判断一本书，要看它的内容！"

妈妈和儿子一有空就去爸爸的坟前。他
们买来鲜花放在墓碑上祈祷，因为他们知道
他一直在守护着他们，"老公，如果你看到
你的儿子变得这么出色，你一定会很高兴
的。"轮到傻瓜西蒙祈祷时，他说："谢谢
你，爸爸，是你派那位睿智的老先生来指点
我的吧。""你爸爸给你派来了一位保护天
使。"他的妈妈回答道，两行热泪夺眶而出。
妈妈和儿子祈祷完之后，心情无比平静，手
拉手走回了家。

傻瓜西蒙对妈妈非常孝顺。她渐渐上了
年纪，决定邀请她寡居的妹妹贝茜来与他们
同住。为了补贴家用，傻瓜西蒙的妈妈和贝
茜姨妈忙着蒸鸡蛋布丁来卖。"这是你奶奶
的秘方。"妈妈和贝茜姨妈告诉傻瓜西蒙说。
虽然妈妈从不抱怨，但他知道她的身体不太

❽ **devoted**
/dɪˈvəʊtɪd/
adj. 挚爱的

❾ **devastate**
/ˈdevəsteɪt/
v. 压倒，使垮掉

consoled[10] Simple Simon. He later took his aunt's advice and told her he would take a year's absence of leave from the school to travel.

Before Simple Simon left, he and aunt Bessie visited his parent's graves. "When I come back, my dearest mother and father, I promise to settle down and raise a family with aunt Bessie's help. She will teach my wife, whomever she may be, how to steam grandma's egg puddings. Mother you remember the kind old gentleman whom you said was my guardian angel sent by father, I will later write stories (no gossip) on my travels dedicating them to you both, my beloved parents. The main cover for all my books will carry the title "MAMA'S EGG PUDDING.""

Moral: A kind word spoken or written is like a magnet[11], which will attract the hearts of men.

好，一天比一天虚弱了。

一天，贝茜姨妈把傻瓜西蒙拉到一边，告诉他说他妈妈患了心脏衰弱症。"她是个好妈妈，你也一直是个好儿子，但是，她可能活不太长了，你要有准备。别太难过，我会尽我所能来照顾她的。"一天夜里，他妈妈的心脏病发作，死神突然降临到了她的头上。傻瓜西蒙痛不欲生，好多天都没有进食。"如果你继续这样下去，你妈妈是不会高兴的。我们知道你想去旅行，现在是时候了。去看看别人是如何生活的，了解一下他们的文化。我会照料农场，继续蒸你妈妈的鸡蛋布丁！"贝茜姨妈安慰着傻瓜西蒙。后来，他采纳了姨妈的建议，告诉她他要离开学校一年去旅行。

傻瓜西蒙动身之前，和姨妈来到父母的坟前。"亲爱的爸爸妈妈，等我回来之后，我保证会安定下来，在贝茜姨妈的帮助下成个家。她会教我的妻子蒸奶奶的鸡蛋布丁。妈妈，你还记得你说是爸爸给我派来的守护天使的那位善良的老先生吧。我会在旅行途中写些故事（不是闲言碎语）送给你们二老，我亲爱的父母。我所有书的主封面都会用《妈妈的鸡蛋布丁》这个标题。"

寓意：所说或所写的一句善言如同磁铁吸引着人们的心灵。

⑩ **console**
/kənˈsəul/
v. 安慰
⑪ **magnet**
/ˈmægnɪt/
n. 磁铁

图书在版编目（CIP）数据

英汉对照·心灵阅读. 5，道德篇/李小艳，陈爱明编译. —北京：外文出版社，2004
ISBN 7 – 119 – 03729 – 3

Ⅰ. 英…　Ⅱ. ①李…②陈…　Ⅲ. 英语 – 对照读物 – 英、汉　Ⅳ. H319.4

中国版本图书馆 CIP 数据核字（2004）第 057283 号

外文出版社网址：
　http://www.flp.com.cn
外文出版社电子信箱：
　info@ flp. com. cn
　sales@ flp. com. cn

英汉对照·心灵阅读（五）

道　德　篇

编　译　李小艳　陈爱明
审　校　林　立

责任编辑　王　蕊　李　湲
封面设计　时振晓
印刷监制　张国祥
出版发行　外文出版社
社　　址　北京市百万庄大街24号　　邮政编码　100037
电　　话　（010）68995963/5883（编辑部）
　　　　　（010）68329514/68327211（推广发行部）
印　　刷　北京中印联印务有限公司
经　　销　新华书店/外文书店
开　　本　大 32 开　　　　　字　　数　150 千字
印　　数　10001 ~ 15000 册　　印　　张　7.75
版　　次　2005 年 10 月第 1 版第 2 次印刷
装　　别　平
书　　号　ISBN 7 – 119 – 03729 – 3/H·1616（外）
定　　价　15.00 元